Marianne E. Meyer
Water Crystals, Messages of the Souls
Using Cosmic Power for a Happy & Healthy Life
A paradigm shift in power production

Producing and publishing:
BoD - Books on Demand, Norderstedt
ISBN 978-3-738-609-776

Some other books by M. E. Meyer:

Spirulina – Survival Food for a New Era
Survival Aid for All Viral Infections
Cranberry Power Fruit
Family Code
Beyond Death
Migrant Birds on Wheels

Cover design,
design, layout, and composition: M. Meyer

Thank you, Deeple, for the translation service and Grammarly for the spelling test

Photo credit:
Thank you for providing the following photo material: E.F. Braun S. 11,13,23,25,34,35,41-44, 47-56,58,62-69,80,81,83,85-87,91-93, NASA 73, B. Simon 114
Cover: R. Taylor, E. Braun

Marianne E. Meyer
Water Crystals, Messages of the Souls
Using Cosmic Power for a Happy & Healthy Life
A paradigm shift in power production

The soul of man is like water:

It comes from heaven.

It rises to heaven

and must come down to earth again,

eternally changing.

Soul of man, how like you are to water!

Destiny of man, how like you are to wind!"

(Johann Wolfgang von Goethe)

TABLE OF CONTENTS

Foreword

A few days before my husband moved into the higher-frequency sphere of existence, he said, "This is no longer my world." To which I replied, "Mine neither." He said, "Oh no, you still will have a lot to go through." It seems that just before we give up earthly existence, we can have a look into the future. Then what came next? I nearly coughed my guts out and lost my sense of smell for over a year. Whether, it was corona, I don't know because at that time, this virus, which later held humanity hostage, was not making many headlines.

Anyhow, the condition of the world today is interpreted even more apocalyptically than at the turn of the millennium when the apocalypse was already the order of the day. And as if virulent microorganisms, water pollution, climate, and environmental disasters combined with the extinction of animal and plant life were not frightening enough, Putin's war threatens nuclear catastrophe.

But are we in fact facing the greatest crisis that has ever come our way - the destruction of the world and humanity? Despite all the depressing news, in some ways, we have changed for the better from before. We have become more open to our fellow human beings. We talk more freely about our preferences, problems, and our dark sides even. We are less and less using the defense mechanism of repression and instead searching deep within our souls for collective solutions that serve us. The recent refugee crisis has made this clear again. We are well on our way to changing the prevailing cult of materialism, prejudice, and greed in our world because other things are more important in the long run. More and more people are calling for a global basic income without conditions. Since we all belong to the same family with 99.9% identical DNA, we should feel the need to ensure that all our relatives can live a dignified life without starving, freezing, or having to leave their homes. A global land income adapted to economic circumstances would make it easier for people to follow their vocation and work according to their desire and love. Too many people pursue jobs that may make them enough money but do not match their talents and do not make them happy.

When we discover our true potential, we can make the world a better place because we work in it. We are also learning more and more about the grand economic secret: the more we give, the more we get. After all, it is a heartfelt gift of love when we give our talent to our fellow human beings.

The message of the water crystals also proclaims unity and love to inspire people to live a life full of the goodness of heart and harmony.

In this book you can learn something about the miracle of the soul. But whether my concept of the soul seems plausible to you is, naturally, entirely up to you. Perhaps you will just be enchanted by the beautiful water crystals or have your own soul stars descend from heaven by the water artists Ernst F. Braun & Sarah Steinmann. If you do your own research, perhaps you will see that we cannot destroy ourselves at all, even if a change of times is upon us. Over the past six years, my late husband has shown me in no uncertain terms that death is by no means the end. I have written three books about our communication. I also became aware we are merely change our frequency when our cat Max lay breathing quietly and deeply in my arms. At the moment of death, his whole body trembled. I was so grateful that Max came to me when he knew he was dying and gave me the opportunity to witness his change of vibration up close. Under VI. WATER TEST WITH MY LATE HUSBAND you will find further evidence of the continued presence of the soul.

The water crystals generated according to Masaru Emoto's method by the above Swiss water artists as so-called soul stars also testify that we live on in the afterlife.

Fifteen years ago, I published the book "Wasser Code Geknackt?" In it, as well as in "How Water Connects Our Worlds" and in my autobiographical novel "Family Code," I introduced you to water crystal pictures as the visual language of souls. My first experiment with neutral water, which informed Ernst Braun with my signature, astonished the latter. Because of his usual 22 frozen water drops, usually only four, rarely eight, can be photographed microscopically. Of my signature 15 pictures succeeded! Only later did I understand the reason for this: Edmond Dembinski, my childhood sweetheart, whom I had the privilege of introducing to art more than half a century ago, died a famous painter. Two paternal friends, Joachim Gestering and Hellmut Hoffmann, Adolph Meyer, my husband's uncle, and Edmond's mother, Wanda von Dembinski, were all gifted painters who are now in the afterlife. That may be one of the reasons why it was easy for me to interpret my water crystals. But also Ernst Braun's water crystal photos, which he generated by informing distilled water with the word "birth trauma" (see page 55 ff.), I could interpret correctly, as well as those of my friends and the cat Max. Therefore, Ernst Braun thought I could also interpret the water crystal photos of his clients. But then the fear of not being good enough crept through all my bones. Maybe you know this too, that you don't trust yourself enough. But since my husband suddenly and unexpectedly said goodbye to me in the afterlife and has already contacted me several times, this might strengthen my self-confidence. Especially for my psychic friend Isabel Bannier-Groß was contacted shortly after by my husband's friend, who had died five years earlier and had proofread my book "Spirulina, Wundernahrung der Zukunft" many years ago. Bolko showed her how I sat at a table and signed the book "Sad News" for my readers.

In the latest experiment in Part V., I informed neutral water with my signature and the photo of my late husband. It would please me if the ingenious crystals could open many windows of enlightenment and bring you into complete vibrational resonance with your heart.

Emoto proved that water responds to sound, writing and language. Brightening thoughts and uplifting music form beautiful crystal structures. With swearing and heavy metal, water crystal pictures show distorted structures. We can better study ourselves with body water and delight ourselves and our neighbors with soft, loving words hence, with heavenly body water crystals. For:

Now is the time for the realization of what is within us.
The cosmic experience of religion is the most powerful
and noblest motive for scientific research.
The most profound and lofty feeling of which we are capable
is experiencing the mystical. Only from this does truly science grow.
He to whom this feeling is foreign, who can no longer marvel
and loses himself completely in awe, is already spiritually dead.
The knowledge that the unfathomable actually exists
and that it reveals itself as the highest truth and the most radiant
beauty of which we can have only a vague idea -
this knowledge and foreboding are at the heart of all religiosity.

(Albert Einstein)

Is this the path to enlightenment?

About sixteen years ago, I began to conduct water crystal photography experiments with Ernst F. Braun and, through the interpretation of the water crystals, to draw attention to the fact that the spiritual world communicates with us through the water. Whenever something decisive happens, such as buying a house in France three years ago (see p. 89), I ask the spiritual water artists for their input. I probably won't live to see my insight revolutionize science. It will take some time because the ruling class is more interested in spreading fear than in revealing the liberating truth. Free people are less likely to be exploited or forced to pay. Individuals with insight are not easily manipulated. But I am convinced that one day people will realize who we genuinely are.

In my book "How Water Connects Our Worlds", I have already pointed out the secret of water's mutability and storage capacity. Inge Schneider, the director of Jupiter Publishing, found my insight that water is the "interface between physical and metaphysical reality" "particularly appealing" in her book review in NET Journal. Through the water crystal photography experiments with Ernst Braun and Sarah Steinmann (www.wasserkristall.ch), I realized that the consciousness that initiates everything also shapes water. The "Atelier für KUNST und Mystik" calls the water crystals with our energy signatures soul stars. I think of them as soul contacts. They often show signs of life or imprinted messages from deceased loved ones. It is a service of love when they communicate with us through each drop of water. But they don't just draw attention to themselves through water crystal photography. They also help us through homeopathy, water refining scalar waves, telepathy, reiki, pendulums and many other projects passed on to me at a higher level of consciousness almost forty years ago. I reported on some of these in "Family Code".

These few lines will hardly suffice to initiate cognitive processes in you. But perhaps the beautiful water crystal pictures in the book will help. In any way, we will find out at the end of our lives what awaits us after our change in the afterlife. That's how I predicted it for my father. He usually just smiled smugly at the Second Face of his loved ones, showing up on my mother's side through all generations. I then asked him to give me a sign. And he did it from the first day of his life in the hereafter, as I will show you below.

I want us all to grasp quickly that soul life, reincarnation, and karma are not esoteric blah blah blah, but the universal law of cause and effect that Paul expresses thus: what a man sows, that he will also reap. Today we say: Karma strikes back. According to this view, there would be no blame of another, no luck or coincidence, but cause and effect, which can be many centuries and embodiments apart. Luck, bad luck, and coincidence merely refer to the law that has not yet been recognized. Every experience, word, and deed, even the smallest detail, is stored in our genes. More specifically, in the junk DNA that makes up more than 90 percent of our genome. I will report on this in Part VII. THE HIDDEN LIGHT IN OUR DNA.

Loosely based on Goethe, I would add that nature makes no mistakes. Errors are always ours. People who are incapable of appreciating creation despise it. Only to the skillful, dedicated, pure, and true does she devote herself and reveal her secrets.

Please pray with me for awareness of this truth will spread quickly and eventually bring world peace. Killing ourselves by hook or crook with weapons of mass destruction, destructive energies, and production is not in our true nature.

I. INTRODUCTION TO WATER ENERGY

The question of the meaning and purpose of life occasionally gives us food for thought. Who turns the wheel of the big picture? Above all, we think about our existence. We possibly want to work with our talents in a pleasant life for the good of our community. Through our thoughts and gifts, we transform the invisible into the visible. When we open ourselves, we give room to chances, which fall upon us easily. This book is also about such coincidences.

How the various shapes and appearances on the frozen drops of water come about is a mystery for most people. Not to me. If you have already admired the water crystal photographs (WCP) by the late Dr. Masaru Emoto and his team, you may also have wondered: What is water trying to tell us? In this work, you will discover that the question should be: Who is speaking through the heavenly wet? The answer may please or frighten you. How comfortable would you be with the thought that we could continue to work as celestial artist painters in the higher dimensions after we shed our physical shells? Children often still have contact with the spiritual world (see page 76 f.). But these spiritual connections are usually lost in the course of their development. When family members who have died find they are confusing the child's environment, they commonly terminate contact.

Quarks or guff?

Was water for you no more than a liquid for brushing your teeth? Then I hope you enjoy admiring the beautiful works of art in the frozen water drops. For me, water crystal photos are no longer a miracle. The metamorphosis of the beautiful red caterpillar willow borer into the nondescript nocturnal flutterer could rival it. Some others, however, will regard the following comments as utter nonsense. But who would have thought years ago that quarks, the tiniest units of matter, could be energy? But whether you want to admire quarks as mediators between the third dimension of objectivity and the fourth dimension of thought and spirit is up to you: physicists and mystics today agree: consciousness initiates all things. Yet many seem to have little to do with the mediating elements. But we know from experience: what we mock today is common knowledge tomorrow. Today we mock the people of the Middle Ages for believing that the sun revolved around the Earth's disk. But when Galileo taught the Copernican system, he almost fell victim to the Inquisition.

The clerics would also have little interest in deciphering the riddle of the formation of water crystals. Especially since neither general chemistry nor physics can answer the question with the resources available: What is water? Half a century of intensive water research and fascinating, sometimes telling working hypotheses leaves the question of the nature of water unanswered. Why? Because science is not comprehensive in its inquiries. Blinkers seem to hinder the search for truth: Why else do only the laws of gravitational force and their consequences apply in today's purely technical approach? Why does established science relentlessly invoke them?

Only a few years ago, I considered the incalculable wet as the most capricious being in the universe: it moves in all directions and overcomes gravity. Solid, liquid or gaseous, it is everywhere. Emoto proved this with his water crystal photography: H_2O responds to sound, pictures, writing and speaking.

Our brains are mainly composed of water. Even we modern humans sometimes still respond to these fine, unconscious vibrations. In my experience, our loved ones in the afterlife often still want to influence us when we receive supersensory perceptions, premonitions and similar spiritual messages.

Multiple studies with interviews of widows, doctors, police officers, and firefighters confirm such contacts after death. Hello from heaven: A new field of research - communication after death confirms that life and love are eternal". At times our loved ones in the afterlife also help us find crucial papers. S. p. 61, 106.

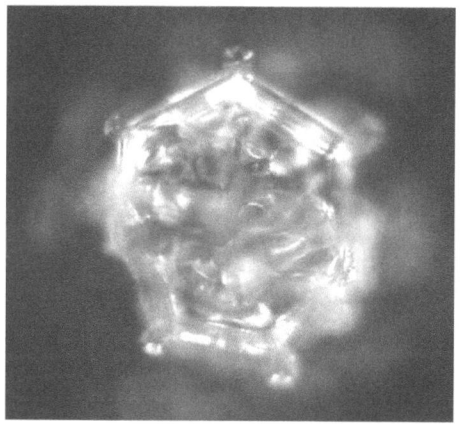 

It's the vibration that counts

Peter Groß, whose GIE water activator won the gold medal at the world's major invention fair in Geneva in 2007, called me to inform me of his success. I had owned his invention for several years. Today, the original Groß devices are sold only under as Aqua-Lyros at aqua-lyros.de. Peter Groß also emailed me two water crystal photos of water from his pipe, the first before and the second after it had gone through his activator. The photos taken before it went through seemed like a hopeless mess. They showed no crystallization. After activation, all of the WCPs were clear with crystallization and seemed separated. Do they tell the sad story of the engineer who supposedly was robbed of his genius? It will not excite him now. Peter Groß left his mortal shell on 9/11/2017, seven months after my husband. Now they don't have to talk on the phone for so long. By the way, most of my deceased relatives and friends died on the 11th, or the cross sum of the day of death is 11. My mother on 1/1/11, my father on 10/1/1998, Peter's mother on 11/11/1987, and my friend Marita on 9/11/01.

I asked the genius engineer who took microscopic photographs of the frozen water droplets, and he gave me Ernst Braun's phone number. I immediately called the water artist in Switzerland. After a stimulating hour-long conversation, Ernst F. Braun offered to inform pure water through my signature and to shine a series of soul stars for me. See pages 19 and 51ff.

We are learning more and more about conscious and unconscious vibrations. Everything that exists is animated and vibrates. Unconsciously, we all communicate with each other, including animals and plants. The latter is the case when we cut leaves from neighboring plants. So soul energy also works between plants and animals.

In one study, researchers connected a measuring device to a plant. When they threw living crabs into a pot of boiling water, the cell system of the plant showed agitation. Using the fly swatter also has consequences: many flies gather to mourn. Everyone suffers when something happens to a member of the community. We also unconsciously communicate with our fellow humans through our soul radar network. Vibrations operate in this soul field. Faraday used the term field and talked about the electromagnetic field. Sheldrake sees morphogenetic fields as a collective astral memory of a non-physical nature. According to him, there is a field pattern behind every structure that first forms, whether it is a thought, an action, or a material object. The more often this structure is formed, the stronger the morphic resonance. These energy fields or grids transmit information beyond time and space. The more sensitive we are or higher our vibrational frequency is, the more data we can receive. It is also possible that a given place has a particularly striking morphogenetic field. Hermosa Beach, for example, could have such a universal consciousness field, for I did "download" an enormous amount of past and future information there. See also p. 44 ff., and Family Code, p. 94 ff. But my 60th gene key may also have played a role, supposedly enabling me to travel through time and space. (Rudd, p. 651)

Sheldrake surmises: It is not only the genetic code that determines heredity. Experiences can also pass on to future generations. Diseases, for example, an intestinal tumor, can thus be family related. If the trigger is recognized at this time and the initial conflict resolved, this will benefit later generations. For example, is a young man killed in an accident, family members may find it hard to cope with the tragic death of their spouse, son, brother, or father. They cannot "digest" it. It sticks in the morphic memory. Field resonance helps some animal species to change their environment. For example, horses around the globe no longer get injured by barbed wire fences since they have become accustomed to them in some countries. (Sheldrake 1993).

Even those who surround themselves with pets can experience the unconsciously working soul energy between humans and animals. If our tomcat Carlo groped to the hallway and sat down next to the door, we knew our better half would arrive a few minutes later. We also know of a dog that announced epileptic seizures: he made himself known in a panic even before his mistress felt the slightest sign of a fit. Oscar, a cat from Providence, RI, USA, known through TV, sensed the approaching death of residents of a nursing home. About three hours before a person passed away, he jumped on the bed and lay there until they breathed their last.

We live and evolve in material and immaterial energy fields: through the energy of the sky or cosmic force and the earth's energy, the telluric power. We all radiate energy that transfers to often-worn objects (crystallized matter).

Psychometrists learn something about the person's character or experiences by scanning such a thing. They can be about the past, the present, or the future. Because according to Einstein, the distinction between past, present, and future is only a particularly persistent illusion. During a seminar on the development of extrasensory perception, I held a ring in my hand and felt heat, cold and more heat. Thinking that the ring's owner had something wrong with her stomach, I advised her to see a doctor. She said, "I already have an appointment for a stomach ailment." If we are observant and guided, we may also be able to avoid accidents. For example, on my way to the market, I suddenly noticed a noise in the car, braked, and drove on carefully. Suddenly, a big green-blue bird that looked like a parrot flew across the road. Without my slowing down, it probably would have collided with my windshield. The whole incident lasted only a few seconds. The sound was then gone again. Did my subconscious cause it, or did the bird's guardian angel intervene?

The intangible is strange and threatening to many. If we allow ourselves guidance, we awaken life-friendly vibrations, and in time we find the invisible neither abhorrent nor disturbing. Perhaps after the training in Part V. USING THE POWER OF THE UNIVERSE, we will soon be able to deal with the soul in the same way as with material energy. Foresight, intuition, clairvoyance, and intuition can be helpful: for one's well-being, the preservation of the environment, and the well-being of one's offspring. The homeopathic method affirms the storage capacity of water.

On Samuel Hahnemann's tracks

What about the vibrations in water? H2O stores information. Hahnemann's experiments proved this: shaken, not stirred. In 2004, the University of Leipzig published an award-winning test tube study entitled "In vitro testing of homeopathic compounds" in the journal "Biological Medicine". Pharmacist Franziska Schmidt, Prof. Dr. Karen Nieber, and Prof. Dr. Wolfgang Süß of the Institute of Pharmacy at the University of Leipzig proved: Solutions of a belladonna extract were physiologically effective even when diluted to the point where there were no molecules of the original substance left in the solution.

The significant thing about the results of this remedy for cramps is that it largely corrects our scientific view of the world. But those who care more about material reality than about the meaning of natural phenomena themselves may have doubts. And those who see their hopes dashed away firmly reject the results. They would not base on objective measurements. But is not the one who heals right? You may ask: What about placebo, the compliant servant of faith? After all, we know that chemically ineffective capsules trigger specific processes in the body: In pain patients, the brain releases endorphins shortly after ingestion (Ter Riet et al. 1998). But not only analgesics can be detected. In patients with Parkinson's disease, the placebo even stimulates the brain to produce the hormone dopamine, which in turn affects coordinated movements.

Faulstich even reports on two experiments with sham surgery. In the first test, sur-geons performed arthroscopies on a subset of patients with knee problems. This surgery requires a small incision under the kneecap. Surgeons can see the problem with a camera inserted through a probe and clean the inside of the knee. In the comparison group, patients had only the incision made. Result: The healing success in the appearance surgery group was as high as in the arthroscopy group. (2006).

In the second experiment, the surgeons inserted a catheter into certain patients with severely calcified heart arteries. In the comparison group, they only simulated the surgery. Again, the group with the sham treatment achieved equally good results. Critical medical experts rightly conclude that many surgical procedures are ineffective and unnecessary.

Can the influence of sham medication be explained by the effect of those who help us from beyond? At least not with the concepts of material science. Are they deceased healers at work here, just as deceased painters draw vibrational images in the water? Could the placebo effect be just another variant of souls communicating with us? In veterinary medicine, veterinarians successfully treat with high potencies of homeopathic remedies. For example, it can cure a specific dog malignancy with only one dose of Hyoscyamus C10000. (Wolff 2014)

What is more rational: to believe that the dog develops self-healing powers through faith and hope or to accept the influence of the spiritual world?

The specific process of homeopathic preparation is vigorous shaking. The diluted solutions are thereby diluted further and further in several steps. During the process, the substance, e.g. gold, phosphorus, or silicon, decreases. A D30 or D200 no longer contains a molecule of the original substance. But the energy of the remedy is driven higher and higher. The ancient physicians still knew that healing occurs through the spirit. For medicine means Medica mente = Heal by the mind.

The imponderable properties of a substance are the intra-atomic energies, which are beyond human imagination due to the homeopathic method of preparation. Transformations related to these nuclear energies occur in the solvent. A material medicinal substance converts into biological energy. When this homeopathic potentiation clears the organic obstacle to balance, the life energy can work once in a proper manner: the damage becomes whole again. However, medicine must attune to the disturbance. If it does not have the same wavelength, it cannot work. We can compare this to a radio tuned to a sure station. That also explains the harmlessness of choosing the wrong drug. Given symptoms must be present as an exit point. Only a reaction makes it possible to find the specific remedy out of the many. If there is no short-term aggravation, it does not work.

The process of homeopathic spillage is incredibly boundless: as if little Johnny in the Azores had tipped a thimbleful of water into the Atlantic Ocean, blown vigorously south, and taken a sample from the Weddell Sea. Yet these homeopathic remedies, informed by the active ingredients, can transmit health-promoting information to the water in our body cells. But how is a hitherto material medicinal substance converted into biological energy?

Are you thinking quarks now, or thought matter as nonsense? We are used to holding on to our habits. Those familiar with energy work know how to interpret feelings. We gain experience through messages from the spiritual world or the body. Skeptics like to suppress what they cannot explain. But skepticism is only a lack of practice. How would we have reacted to radio waves 120 years ago? The claim that one could sound children's choirs or brass concerts by the touch of a button would have met with jeers. Not to mention e-mailing and video messaging over the Internet.

How is water informed?

Masaru Emoto managed to promote light work with water crystal photos. The soul stars Ernst F. Braun took from the sky shone a whole sea of light into me. Like the Japanese team, the Swiss photographed frozen water droplets. Because of my metaphysical experiences, it would have been immediately clear to me: Water is a medium for the other world. But how is the wet stored with information?

E. Braun attached the piece of paper with my signature to a glass of distilled water. See p. 41. He filled 22 Petri dishes with one drop each of the informed H_2O and froze them at -30°C. The freezer is in a geomantically undisturbed location. After a few days, he sent me 15 WCPs. At first, I thought they were just beautiful. But with each new look at my soul stars, I discovered new old things: most of them reflect my live!

What is this water wonder trying to tell us? What or who is behind it? Because of the in persona messages and I had previously had paranormal experiences with deceased relatives and acquaintances, it soon dawned on me who the water was informing: Our dead! The essential wet seems to be a medium for souls, which explains its unpredictability. Because they exist at a higher Vibration level, we do not see them, even though they are constantly around us. My grandmother was not telling me a fairy tale when she said, Your grandfather in heaven always sees what you are doing. Friedrich Jürgenson's explanation of contacting the afterlife in "Sprechfunk mit Verstorbenen" (Radio Telephony with the Deceased) confirmed my suspicions. But more on that later.

My soul stars, which reflected pleasant experiences, formed beautiful crystal shapes. The crises in my life came out as barely formed or split crystals or showed a broken heart. I first took the above WCP, which resembled a colon, as a warning to think about an investigation. After three weeks of headaches, I was lounging in the shallow bath water when the penny dropped. The essential wetness led, like once Archimedes: Eureka! Suddenly I remembered who the painter of the colon crystal might have been: Jürgen, my husband's friend who died in an accident! Because we had to find out by now: His daughter, Peter's daughter-in-law, had been diagnosed with a tumor in her colon during a preventive medical check-up. The surgeon removed it in a successful operation.

Her sister and other family members also suffered from a growth in the colon. You may be wondering: What is a foreign colon doing in my soul star? Did we need to be made aware that everything would be all right? Because this WCP shows a beautiful crystal. Did Peter's friend use the medium water to calm his daughter or to help her get over the loss of her grandmother?

The "3" with the word volume in the upper third of the WCP represents another prophecy: Three surgeries had been necessary because of complications. Do you find the idea that souls communicate with us grotesque? Then watch the video of the mediumistic painter Antonio Gasparetto, which you can find at the following link. He paints old masters in a trance with his hands and feet. Better said, the latter use him as a channel to tell us: Look, we still exist! Do the souls of Dr. Sauerbruch and colleagues also work through spirit surgeons? The American television host Oprah Winfrey has presented some of them. Who knows how many projects the spiritual world connects with us still?

www.youtube.com/watch?v=URM8KGpjztE

As you can see, Antonio paints at a furious pace. He chooses the right color from the palette or the paint box without hesitation. After a few minutes, Antonio finished a Modigliani, Rembrandt, or Toulouse-Lautrec. He said he is in touch with the Old Masters and leaves his hands and feet to them. There are also sometimes true masters of art creating the water crystals.

Soul of man, how like the water you are!

Goethe could have been even more specific about the mystery of water, sparing humanity perhaps much suffering. But geniuses need not necessarily be people of courage. After all, the genius Goethe regarded H_2O as a medium for transmitting messages from the ether. We will only one day know exactly how this works when we try to contact our loved ones who are still alive. It would be better for the survival of our species if we all knew that we do not die. If we expect to populate our beautiful planet with other bodies, we should be more careful using it.

Now how can we approach the ubiquitous wetness? What do we know so far about water? Two hydrogen atoms and one oxygen atom form an H_2O molecule. The electrically charged particles draw their probable orbits around the atomic nuclei. These electron orbits overlap and hold the molecule together. Likewise, the force fields act like an adhesive that chains the neighboring molecules. That is how engineer Otto Dutschk explains the formation of water's incomparable soul energy fields. Just as it fluctuates together here, the water soul of our earth also fluctuates. And so the soul of the essential wetness vibrates in our organism. "The water atoms take the characteristic form, so to speak, the energy field of the soul H_2O by the interaction of their force fields. So we can consider other chemical formulas and blueprints in nature as standardized forms of the soul energy, so to speak."

Dutschk shows how electrons form structures in their various vibrational forms. The soul energy fields are already present at the roots of being and create countless alternative possibilities to build networks. Thus, billions upon billions of individual soul energy fields have formed in the unfolding of nature. Through their unified harmonious oscillation with each other, they form one uncontrollable whole of soul energy - the cosmos (1999, p. 151). This infinite pole of the original soul is where we all interact. The more equal vibrations we allow, the more consciousness we develop. Disharmony blocks the power of cognition. Harmony expresses guidance through the elemental will. When we accept and follow the lead, we feel safe and radiate the joy of life.

Our soul field functions like a receiver network. For example, when we lean against a tree, the tree's vibrations connect with our own. We usually feel refreshed. Our soul field is subject to fluctuations in field form depending on

21

how we feel. Whether we sit cozy in the bathtub or walk through icy slush, we are foaming hot with anger or happy as a lark. The feeling is nothing but vibration. Ergo, there can be no such thing as an eternally constant sensation, only change. Because water constantly changes state. Pleasant and unpleasant alternate incessantly.

Can we influence this change or control our emotions? You bet we can! Emoto showed us. Let's think of a pleasant situation from the past, such as an unforgettable kiss. Our turn toward the sensation amplifies its vibrations. It quickly dominates our consciousness. Let's feel what our senses perceive: Smell, taste, light, and color: all are vibrations. If we perceive this moment specifically sensory, not only the brain is involved in this act of perception, but the whole body system. Now, when one sensation enters consciousness, other perceptions disappear. Now it is the will's turn, then the body's. We act. The body or body water is a mediator for the realization of the interplay between will and sensation. Babies consist of almost 90% H_2O. Intuitively they understand everything. Could the spiritual world communicate better with them through higher storage capacities? Our lives would probably be less confusing if we trusted our feelings more. Did our ancestors realize that water was more than an element for drinking, brushing teeth, and watering flowers? Would it have been much more in the consciousness of primitive man? Whether it is sacred or just a reservoir, we can argue about that. In any case, one thing is for sure: without H_2O, there is no life.

Many of the following crystals have hexagons, crescents, and keyholes. Ernst Braun once emailed me a crystal showing an enthroned Buddha surrounded by hexagons with a crescent moon and keyhole. Hexagons symbolize the honeycomb, indicating stability and reliability, traditionally strong values. The crescent moon symbolizes the feminine, mysterious power that is intuitive and not rational. The keyhole also represents the feminine. I would interpret it this way: We are facing a change, and coming to the heart will serve the mind. Do we currently have so many wars, earthquakes, floods, and volcanic eruptions because we are about to transition into the age of peace, freedom, and virtue, like the finale of a fireworks show? We had better all make an effort to quickly master the task of reconciling our impressionable minds with the wise heart.

The Saggy water crystal photo describes my personality: Although I keep a cool head in dangerous situations, I tend to react stubbornly or lose my nerve when searching for my key, for example. This funny little doll, where the head should have been, would appear to portray absent-mindedness or childishness.

If you want to do your own research with water crystal photos, please contact:

Atelier für KUNST und Mystik – Ernst F. Braun & Sarah Steinmann
CH-3628 Uttigen, Eichenweg 8
ernst_braun @ bluewin.ch
wasserkristall.ch

II. CRYSTALLIZED CONSCIOUSNESS

Water has a memory influenced by the consciousness of the soul. Masaru Emoto's work shows how water is affected by the environment, thoughts, words, music, and emotions.

Emoto's icy miracles

Some 200 years after the founding of homeopathy, Masaru Emoto made us receptive to the message of the essential elixir with his water crystal photographs. For years, the Japanese alternative doctor researched H_2O through vibrational measurements. In America, he found a device that could transfer information to water. He used it to develop a cure. But his idea of freezing water and then photographing it caught the world's attention. The mesmerizing photographs in his book "The Message of Water" speak volumes: energy reveals itself in ice crystals through wave motion and vibration. H_2O responds to thoughts, words, writings, and images ...

According to Emoto's research, the word "thank you" has the most positive effect on water and the environment overall. "Arigato," thank you in Japanese, was also the water researcher's last word when he died on Oct 17, 2014.

The scientific world does not know everything about the changeable and unpredictable primordial substance that holds all knowledge. Under lab conditions, it became clear that attempts to obtain uniform explanations failed. What keeps researchers from shifting their fields of inquiry into the spiritual realm? It would be ingenious if the reports about the water crystals in the next chapter could spark new studies.

Masaru Emoto, when he tried to inform H_2O with a photograph of Mother Teresa, got vastly different images of the photographed ice cubes. The critics blamed the fact that he chose what he found most characteristic as a subjective view. Why so many diverse pictures come to light became clear to me only through the work of Ernst F. Braun, as you can see later.

Some of Emoto's experiments suggest that we can protect ourselves from electro-smog, provided we carry love and gratitude in our hearts. Because we then form beautiful crystals in the bodily water. How we can generate loving and gratefulness, structure water, and strengthen our immune system is explained in detail in my self-help book for perfect immunity protection and in "Wunderwesen Wasser".

How can we structure our body water?

Emoto's water crystal pictures suggest: Through good thoughts, harmonious music, uplifting literature, and exciting television programs, we can activate our body water. We can also structure the water in our food by listening to soft music and uplifting thinking. Have you ever wondered why the same food sometimes feels delicious but at other times is heavy on your stomach? The mood during preparation makes all the difference. So Emoto's discovery hardly comes as a surprise: happy thoughts and uplifting music, such as classical music, evergreens, chansons, gospel, or folk, form crystalline structures (cluster = formation of heaps of H2O molecules). Hard rock, heavy metal, and songs with anapaestic beats show destroyed crystals.

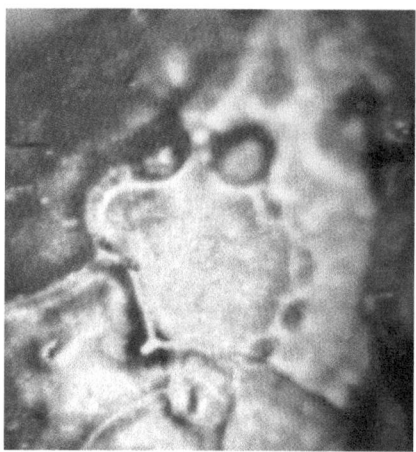 

Since we can cleanse polluted water through positive influences, the assumption is obvious: Any vibration affects our body water and, thus, our being. So we have a choice to structure our body water. We can salt our soup with dismal thinking and generate disharmony with shrill tones. On the other hand, we can bring the inner juice into a higher vibration: with sonatas by Bach or catchy tunes by Elvis or the Beatles. Through such musical works, we balance our organ system. So praying before meals also makes sense. Likewise, if something makes you mad, it would be better not to cook or eat anything.

Emoto's first picture book shows the brilliant hexagonal structure of the previous page. The photo to the left of water from what must have been a contaminated reservoir shows a hideous image resembling a festering ulcer. After head priest Reverend Kato had subjected the lake to a soul purification experiment in the form of meditation, the researchers generated this beautiful water crystal picture.

We can also strengthen our nervous system and harmonize body fluids with deep abdominal breathing. After the deep inhalation, we tighten all the muscles and think of desirable and positive things. You may want to consider: Don't we learn an extraordinary amount from the so-called negative? Of course, you can also set the autopilot. The soul knows what is best for the vehicle. And ultimately, our feelings, fear, insecurity, and happiness are just factors of our chemical composition, which is constantly changing. So, the only certainty in our lives is change.

What makes us so unique?

In the flesh, our consciousness collects experiences rather than in the spiritual dimensions. They record as information in our so-called junk DNA and a kind of cosmic library. We feel about every vibrating cell already in the womb. Water absorbs information in every body cell, stores it, and the junk DNA transmits it. Our environment, people, furniture, paintings, plants, each smell, sound, and stone affect our body water. Old clutter weighs us down and can lead to discomfort. A mixture of tableware, wicker, fabric, whole galleries of closets, or mountains of brochures and photographs affects us all. Who hasn't experienced a tremendous energy boost from thorough tidying? Energy stagnated by clutter can flow freely again after clearing. As we clean our environment and body of water, our mind can become clear also, and our existential self can resurface. As we further free ourselves from doubt and guilt, buried intuition can resurface, and our individuality can come back to life. It occurs to me that I was particularly intuitive in Hermosa Beach when we were starting over in the U.S. without the junk.

Anyone who has filled out the classical homeopathy questionnaire knows how differently we react to wind, humidity, temperature, air pressure, thunderstorms, and other atmospheric conditions: Some tolerate warm weather better, others cold, dry, or wet. The region we grow up in is also influential: My Ph.D. mother in gerontology, Anitra Karsten from Finland, felt fine in gray weather. I find cold wind terrible, and dry 25° is a blessing. We also have a different feeling, waiting alone, in the dark, before or during menstruation, and at certain times of the day or year. We cry on certain occasions: some at music, others at reproaches, some for no reason. We also tolerate different foods. And we change throughout our lives in weather sensitivity, tastes, or habits.

Considering Emoto's results, individual impregnations become even more complex: we can imagine something about purifying our body water. It makes sense to sharpen our sense organs, ergo perceptual awareness. Through the WCP of the Japanese and his followers, we can get an idea of how to make the crystals of our body water glow: for example, through pure waters, rest, Reiki, pure, loving thoughts, singing, praying, moving, yoga, laughter, dancing, stones, Bach flowers, Schüßler salts ...

Water as medium and truth detector

What if all truth could come to light through water crystals? Years ago, Masaru Emoto's research purpose was to produce water crystal images anywhere in the world without refrigerating waters. He said a prototype of a device connecting to a PC already existed (Zeitgeist 4/2000, p.48). Since then, I have read every other work by Emoto and wondered why he never again mentioned the device. I think this was another project of the spiritual world, like the scalar-wave device that helps us get or stay healthy. Perhaps Emoto was also threatened or bribed, just like the many genius inventors who are a thorn in the side of the energy companies with their free-energy projects.

Wouldn't it be wonderful if we could all enlist the help of our higher-frequency bodies or the spiritual world? For example, in shopping, choosing food beneficial to our organism is comparable to commuting, only more precise. Or in choosing medicines and types of therapy. After all, many of them make us more sick than healthy. Or, to quote the British writer Aldous Huxley:

Medical science has made such tremendous progress
that there is hardly a healthy human left.

The truth detector would also pick up less benevolent vibrations from a counterpart and warn against further contact due to lack of crystal formation. Sensitive people feel it anyway. But even they sometimes reach their limits: for example, when they become agitated by transference phenomena, they no longer trust their intuition. We often read expectations, fears, or ideas into a person's behavior or traits originally meant for another person. A WCP device might help if, for example, a merchant's smile reminded us of someone who has deceived us. If it showed a beautiful crystal, we would be at ease. A dark low-frequency image might alert us and arouse our suspicion. However, I doubt that a WCP device can avoid all wrong decisions. After all, many experiences are part of our destiny or are in our genes.

What helps us become empty and see clearly?

Who will disagree when I say nothing is what it seems at first glance? We constantly experience how people manipulate reality and ruthlessly exploit it psychologically and physically.

Not only scientists, governments, and the media lie to us. Everywhere facts are falsified and groundbreaking works suppressed. We are short-changed and fooled. Yet from the cradle, we want to gain more knowledge. When we observe young children, this becomes very clear.

Especially when it comes to the meaning of life and man's role in cosmic drama, we seem to be on the wrong track. But emptied by meditation, silence, or fasting, we reach a higher vibration. Even if we swing the walking stick, we can approach the core of our being. It is not necessarily Jacob's Way that leads to humility. My brother-in-law, who crossed the South Atlantic a few years ago, all alone, in his Spartan racing catamaran, may have been also more receptive to the essential. The solitude and extreme situations lead us to the source of our being. No one can fool us so quickly. We all know who we are and where we come from. We are only more or less forced to develop correspondingly effective defense mechanisms and rationalize emotional things. Since we inhabit a body and live in a world where miracles seem impossible, only rational actions are in the foreground, which we put forward as motives for acting.

But since we all network on the World Wide Web, it has become increasingly difficult to suppress the truth. More and more people are expanding their perceptual awareness and realizing that the physical world is not the only reality in the universe. The physicist and chemist Prof. Dr. Milan Rýzl stated in his 2005 parapsychological research report: "Our physical world of matter is only a part of a higher world that is independent of space, time and matter. Man lives on after death in this spiritual universe of higher dimensions. And he does so as something of this spiritual entity we call the soul."

The message of the soul stars presented here also indicates that these souls of the departed can contact us through the water.

Initiation by my own experience

As I considered writing a major work on various natural healing methods, I wanted to know if my debut work would be successful. So in the late 1980s and early 1990s, during a séance and a channelling, I asked the same question of two different mediumistic people. Dirk Benedict's book inspired me: Confessions of a Kamikaze Cowboy: A True Story of Discovery, Acting, Health, Illness, Recovery, and Life. The actor, known for his role as Face in the series *The A-Team*, was able to cure himself of his incurable prostate cancer caused by his "3-meat-meal diet," using only a strict macrobiotic diet. Both mediums gave me the same message: they did not see thick books but ten small ones.

Eight years later, my spiritual honeymoon was over, and as I wrote my field report, the words of the psychics came back to me: Indeed, my first ten books were not thick. Although, the 200 or so pages of the "Family Code" in large format could well become a 400-page book.

I hope this book can help you develop and strengthen a sense of oneness with everything. For our development and consciousness, we better explore the world of spiritual beings. The exchange so far has occured through mediumship, automatic writing, telepathy, truth dreams, clairvoyance, clairaudience, or psychometry. In the future, we will also be able to communicate through the medium water. That is what the water crystal photos suggest. Only a few around me seem to realize what is going on and what it could mean for us. It was recently, when I proofread the book "The Golden Path", that I realized that my higher purpose in this life is to bring this awareness to my fellow human beings. As a teacher in life's work, I have four lineages related to the dissemination of knowledge: divine will, intention, passion, and IQ. For clarification, here is an excerpt from the above book:

"Line 2 - the brilliant mind – provocative

Is your IQ broken by the subject in the second line, it shines with the beauty of its genius. It is a mind that never ceases to astound, because it continues to make quantum leaps. The brilliance of the two-line comes into its own here in this atmosphere. These kinds of minds are the great researchers of the mental plane. They lead the human mind to the limits of its understanding. That is a way of thinking that involves both left-sided logic and the right hemispheric vision of the brain. Such spirits often seem to be far ahead of the times in which they live. They are original and creative minds who often make groundbreaking breakthroughs. They find themselves in almost every field of human endeavor, from the sciences to art and music. The twin mind is not just thinking – it involves a highly expressive and creative life. These are people made to be in the spotlight" (Rudd 2018, p. 185).

If you also want to learn about your purpose or higher destiny in the present life, you can get your hologenetic profile at the following link. Just enter your place of birth, date, and time.

https://genekeys.com/free-profile/

You'd be surprised how much you can learn about yourself. What if we all followed our golden path? How would it affect science, art, and religion? What would it do to power structures? Would it create transparency in other areas as well? In any case, I will make a special effort to unravel the mystery of how we can inform water. Knowing how energy, will, and wave motion work, we can better understand the images. Some animals and isolated people of intuition can even see vibrations or energy fields.

In this book, you can marvel at all the expressive illustrations with your own eyes. Many people understand just what they can see with their own eyes. And even then, we all understand something different, which brings us back to Paul Watzlawick's question: How real is reality? Does it arise only through subjective perception and, therefore, can never be understood as an objective? My professor of pedagogy Ernest Jouhy spoke of the double refraction of consciousness. Let us sensitize our mental perception so that even science will finally see: the sole claim of the oft-cited objectivity stands on shaky foundations. Christian Morgenstern puts it this way:

There are no secrets per se, only non-initiates of all degrees.

What is the objection to drawing on one's own experience? As subjects, of course, all our standpoints are subjective. Then how can there be a neutral point of view, i. e. absolute objectivity? We are unique individuals and if we listen more to our inner voice, the soul's wisdom will guide us.

How do we use wisdom in the unconscious?

Unconscious action is not uncommon, even if it sometimes seems mysterious to us. Who warns us when meeting strangers or in traffic? We may consider it fortunate when we follow our first intuition and choose the right path. But what is behind it? Is it our unlimited self that strives to keep us on the best and most pleasant course in life, or is it the telepathic efforts of our loved ones in the afterlife? Either way, far too often, the mind takes over, distracting us. But if we trust in the guidance of the soul(s), not everything will always happen the way we want it to happen, but it is always the way that is right and important for us in a particular situation.

You can create pleasant coincidences yourself. With thoughts and feelings, you shape the field of your soul energy so that you experience more joy in life. For example, if I want to go to town by car to shop in a store, I prepare myself as follows: Because of limited parking space, I visualize a suitable parking space. At the same time, I imagine the area around the store exactly: I see a woman leaving the bakery next door, smelling the scent of freshly baked bread. Just then, a van comes out of a parking lot. I park and find the item on sale that I want to buy. You will be surprised at how effectively field forms of soul energy help us master everyday life: especially when we visualize pleasant things, even without cause. By visualizing joyful events, we prefabricate that present imprint in the unconscious. But what if our cells build up harmful vibrations, and these become a habit?

Do you know this? You have not paid attention to where you are going, and you don't know where you are: It's cold and dark. Panic seizes you. Your now dominant sympathetic nervous system produces stress acids because of the upset. Or it happens because you have misplaced your key. You run around headless, search the whole apartment, but can't find it. In that case, you stop, take a deep breath and calm down. When the parasympathetic nervous system kicks in, you can contact your Higher Self or Spirit Self. After a few deep breaths and perhaps a few more sips of water, you usually remember what direction you came from or where you put the key. When you take in the unconscious promptings, you set the course for optimal options: You can direct your life a bit easier and generate more love for life. If you trust your inner wisdom, you will find water and trees, even in the desert, perhaps even with yourself.

This example shows how important it is in our time, characterized by permanent stress, to cushion the fear of the future triggered by terror, wars, economic bankruptcies, and job worries with an alkaline diet. If we eat more greens and unwind by singing, dancing, and meditating, we can get a grip on our over-acidification, which is common today. But we lay the best foundation through the love in our hearts or from a four-legged friend. When our heart smiles, we can perfect our water crystals.

Below you will find many pictures of the crystalline structures of H_2O. As you already know, information about the acoustic, chemical, or electromagnetic frequency patterns can imprint on the excellent store of energetic vibrations. But whether you agree with me that the painters of the water crystals are our loved ones in the afterlife, enjoying themselves on the astral plane without the stress of physical life, is up to you. You could still be one of the pioneers in this field if you would make experimenting with water crystal pictures your hobby.

Ernst F. Braun is happy to accept exciting orders. You can enjoy very personal works of art or unique wall decorations. The only important thing would be that you count yourself among those whose critical sense is not too sharpened. Because if you have retained the directness of imagination, this can be very exciting. When you are not indoctrinated in a particular direction, you are more willing to acknowledge unexpected facts, however surprising they may be. If you want to do science, you had better not hope for government loans. Instead, you have to reckon with being ridiculed. But with perseverance, self-confidence, faith in the cause and one's talent, as is well known, one reaches any goal. In any case, the beings working in or with the water seem ready to reveal their secret.

III. IMAGERY OF THE SOULS

> Radiantly beautiful soul stars show me true power.
> They touch delicate strings and fill my heart with joy.
> The souls give comfort and feelings of bliss.

Soul stars - crystallized energy

How do we receive energetic messages? Sometimes it is simply a feeling that tells us this is as it should be and not otherwise. Sometimes we are warned through prophetic dreams and visions. Clairaudience is also about instructions from our unlimited Higher Self or other souls. The soul stars described here are probably mostly the work of souls who have passed away. They seem to understand all our languages and be able to read our thoughts and writings. Their transmitted messages attest to their existence. But whether they acquire their knowledge through our natural frequencies, by observation, by consul-ting the cosmic chronicle, or in some other way and transmit it to the waters, we will probably only find out when we one day approach our native regions again.

Even without knowing exactly how it works, we can use activated H2O to our advantage. It contains all the frequencies of light. When we drink or bathe in this Lightwater, it emits exactly the vibrations we need at that moment to balance our organism (Meyer 2002).

If you want to make your judgments about the water painters, intuitive Swiss Ernst F. Braun and his daughter Sarah Steinmann will be happy to bring you their soul stirrings from heaven. Dare to do your experiment. You can have water crystal photos taken of yourself, your loved ones, pets, springs, rivers, lakes, fountains, construction sites, or your tap water. There seems to be nothing not to be viewed objectively. Or rather: In water, all vibrations are copied and converted into visible form. But you may not even like what comes to light. After all, if you know your partner, children, or pets a little, that's one thing. But as far as an alien making a caricature of his spouse's essence in front of you, that can be thought-provoking.

Nothing seems to escape the soul painters. If only everyone were aware that we are being watched! Who would lie and cheat if we firmly expected the consequences? Who would rape and murder if they knew they would have to make up for the transgressions?

The water artist on a journey

When I called Ernst F. Braun, I had just read Hape Kerkeling's book on his trip on the Way of St. James, which Shirley MacLaine had traveled years earlier in 28 days. That's how we got talking about pilgrimages. The Swiss has mastered the middle Way of St. James, the so-called Power Line, from his hometown: about 2,200 km! He says about himself:

The so-called Way of St. James is much older than Christianity. The Christians merely revived it and placed their cathedrals (the corpus of power) at places of power. The Way does not end in Santiago, but in Finisterre.

What does it mean to wander the world all alone? When a person roams for months, it becomes wonderfully quiet inside. Then the senses are seismic, and he can work his miracles. In Ernst F. Braun's book "Wasserkristalle. Zauberwelt auf gefrorenen Wassertropfen," I found the space pictures particularly exciting. Mr. Braun did not answer my question about how he obtained

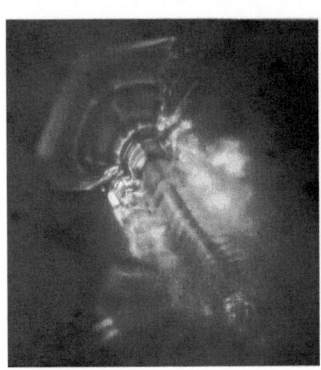
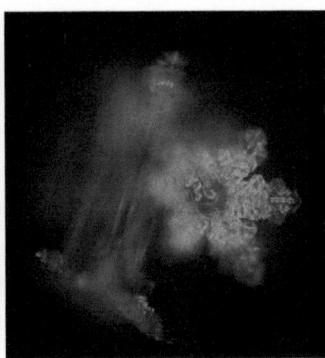
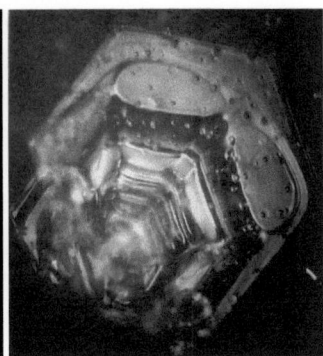

them. Admittedly, this enticed my imagination to make air jumps: If you spend months wandering through desolate lands, you can end up somewhere completely different. When I asked Mr. Braun about the water artist's Camino de Santiago story, he said that few people would be interested in his version of "I'm off then." Still, I found his experiences remarkable. Are they even related to water? After all, a middle-aged man is still composed of 60-65% water:

When I walked the path from Burgistein CH to Santiago, I did focus on empti-ness. I don't remember much about the first 500 km to Le Puy. Everything revolved around me. Then, along with nature, it got better and better.

In Spain, I arrived at my place, and I still remember almost every step. Also the so-called emptiness came in more and more often. My mind, I mean, thinking, sometimes rolled away like a carpet from the floor. Then there was being alone. It was lovely to rest without thoughts. The separation between me and nature, the tree, the path, the bird, etc., which the mind no longer names, but which the feeling level only perceives, dissolves.

Of course, there is also a possibility of addiction behind this. Perhaps this is one of the reasons why people keep going on pilgrimages. The question then arises afterward: where are all the religions, moral concepts, differences, etc., when the thinking apparatus stands still?

How I came to soul communication

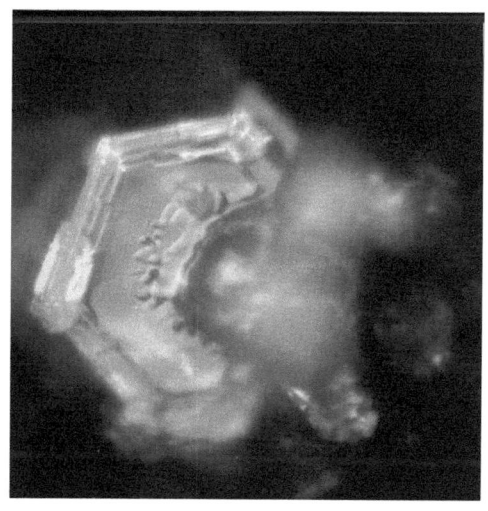

Who are the beings who paint vibra-tional images in painting the water? When I discovered Ernst Braun's WCP of a farmer's spring in his book, I asked: Was that the farmer from Lucerne who dug the spring? Could the senior's profile be a self-portrait?

Without reading "Voice Transmis-sions with the Deceased," I probably would have believed that the water created the image. But now I can imagine it like Friedrich Jürgenson's tape contacts with the afterlife. While listening to recorded bird sounds, the opera singer and painter heard the voice of his deceased mother. But the dead mix their electromagnetic waves into our radio waves: Scientists, radio experts, and sound engineers have found no plausible technical explanation for this phenomenon. The head of the Parapsychological Institute at the University of Freiburg, Prof. Hans Bender, confirmed its existence. You can listen to the voices at:

www.vtf.de and vtf.de/schweden.shtml.

Friedrich Jürgensen's mother had addressed her son by his nickname: "Friedel, can you hear me? That's Mammi." Later, acquaintances who had long since died or had just passed away also called. Radio contacts were participated in by musicians, singers, and actors trained during their lifetimes. The deceased replaced the voices of the singers in the broadcasts with their own. Through word metamorphoses, the latter sent personal messages. Now you may be asking: why bother? But what if one day, you slip out of your physical shell and discover that you still exist? Wouldn't you then also want to inform your next of kin?

So it was with my father's uncle, who died while I was visiting home in the late 1980s. We were living in California at the time. The night before the funeral, I had the following dream: our German-American tax consultant Edi visited us in our apartment in Hermosa Beach and marveled at my creation in oil paint. She said, the town hall of Michelstadt! I had just been to the Christmas market. I said, maybe we have acquaintances from each other. Edi said, I know Heinz Wutz. Surprised, I exclaimed, that's my father's cousin. I told my mother about the dream.

At the funeral, Heinz sat directly across from me. What could be more logical than his late father had given me the prophetic dream? Or did my soul, which had escaped from the body during sleep, make contact with him? A few weeks later, Edi came to our apartment for the first time. Before that, she had only visited us in the car storage at LAX Airport. Everything happened as if in a dream because when our soul penetrates other dimensions on its nocturnal walks, it can experience everything that is, was, and will be. Only in the dense third dimension do we discern past, present, and future. In space-time, these times are fantasy.

Compassion from deceased loved ones

The souls living in higher dimensions do not just paint in the water to communicate with us. They also make use of mediumistic people. Shirley MacLaine's experiences with mediumistic painter Luiz Antonio Gasparetto, pictured above, suggest that Old Masters work with mediums. When the actress visited Antonio, he channeled Toulouse-Lautrec. As the latter painted Shirley, he used not only Gasparetto's hands but also his voice, saying he had painted Shirley once before in his life: as a courtesan. So it's no wonder she did so well in the part of the girl Irma la Douce. It earned her an Oscar nomination. That the Oscar-winning and best-selling author mentioned in her book "Going Within, A Guide for Inner Transformation".

Genius originates in knowledge
acquired in past lives.

As I said, it took a while to realize that I have known the artists at work on my water crystal photos: for example, Jochen Gestering, a family friend to whom I owed my first contact lenses: He saw me playing badminton with star glasses when I was 15. He, who lost a leg in World War II, understood how a girl feels with thick glasses where a dum-dum bullet would ricochet off. I was very embarrassed and wore the glasses only at home and in school. The Gesterings always had an open house. Although I couldn't quite catch the elaborate conversations of assembled artists and teachers at the time, I felt accepted. When I was 19, I met Edmond Dembinski. For a year and a half, we were like lovebirds in the lap of his artistic family.

One sister was a stage designer, the other a painter. Edi's mother, Wanda von Dembinski, painted a portrait in oil that resembled a photo in two hours: not always to delight the clients. Wanda managed to reflect something of the character and inner truth. But who likes to look into the eyes of his shadow?

Not long after Edi fulfilled his mother's wish for a colorfully painted coffin, he slipped out of his long body in 2002. Also, the painter Hellmut Hoffmannn could have made some water crystal art. He had worked as an art teacher at the Odenwald School. I had a lively correspondence with the Michelstadt native when we lived in the US for ten years. I like the thought that the many soul stars are probably gifts from these painters.

The water crystal photos generated from the picture of our cat Max (page 51 ff.), who came from the animal shelter in North Hollywood, also document his 13-year history. If these are from my late painter friends, they may have obtained the data through astral memories. Or they may visit us occasionally to get the information through observation. Either way, the water crystal photos show us that there are more things between heaven and earth than school wisdom teaches us.

As much as Friedrich Jürgenson collected tape voices, I collected countless supernatural experiences in L. A. What moved me most was the opening of the family secret passed on a more spiritual level. My great-grandfather had abandoned my great-grandmother with a 2-month-old problem. But the love child was born in marriage because an honorary savior in the New Apostolic congregation married her. In the early 1990s, I was determined to find out where relatives of my great-grandfather, who had emigrated to the USA in 1902, might still be living. But the time was not yet ripe for tracing the possible descendants of the ancestor who came from the Hanau area. Will I ever have the chance to identify my great-grandfather, who appeared to me as a ghost, in the photo album of the still strange family? Will I ever meet one of the Victors who supposedly settled in enchanting Carmel, California? Little did I know then that a famous great-aunt of my mothers also lives in Carmel. Although 35 years ago, a fortune teller said I was related to Doris Day. Had I believed better, Doris could have met her three great-nieces who visited me in Encino, California. In my book "Family Code", among other things, I wrote about my rapprochement experience in Carmel.

Anyway, as the heavenly messages flow, I will gratefully accept the guidance and am anxious to see where the waves will take the book, my readers, and me. In any case, the spiritual world seems to be contacting us to confront the public with irrefutable facts. It uses various channels: Some spiritual beings contact us by radio or PC, and others reach us in dreams. Or they contact us with their odor. That also happened on Sep 3. 1998, when I sat at the computer, and my grandmother's fragrance touched me as if she were standing behind me. She probably wanted to draw my attention to a special event. Possibly, the page with my interview rattled through the press at the printing and publishing house. The following morning, my mother called and said, Today you are the star of the newspaper: an interview of almost one page with a large color photo of you and your book. I told my mother about the smell experience. To which she said, Strangely, when I read the article, I felt as if she had been looking over my shoulder. Maybe she had contact with my father at that time because 28 days later, she took him home. He has certainly been aware of the date of his death, as his annual file read: to the end of Sep 98. On Oct 1, he left his remains behind him. Peter also said shortly before his death, "I don't think I'll live past 75. I said, "I don't think so, your father was 76 fifty years ago, and you will live at least ten more years.

Indeed, Peter has already contacted me several times: through visual contact, out-of-body, and telephone exchanges, as well as physical phenomena, mainly related to electricity, as you can read in my book "Beyond Death". That the spiritual world can communicate with us through electricity, Toulouse-Lautrec also mentioned in a 1981 video made by the spirit painter Gasparetto: youtube.com/watch?v=bWpc71VKiDI

Have you experienced any unusual things yourself? E. g. on the PC: it's like it takes on a life of its own. Or something is deleted, and afterward, when the anger passes, we realize: It was just as well. A few years ago, a foreword of a book accidentally flew away. When I opened the file, only blank sheets appeared! Quickly I pulled out the USB flash drive to transfer the saved text. But as soon as I opened the file, the text also disappeared! On the computer there was another version stored from 6 days earlier. My husband took me in his arms regretfully. Years ago, I would have been totally upset by such an accident. But then I said, Well, never mind, that's how it should be. Soon after, I wrote a completely new beginning.

Being guided not only means less stress but also better results. It is best that we remain open to everything that happens with all wireless connections. Because this is where our loved ones in the afterlife can contact us: It only depends on the wavelength. And they seem to be very fond of connection, evident from the experiences described here, in my other books and in many other works. The way we currently mistreat the earth could also be an urge to connect. It is up to us how we want to deal with it. In the dawning age of Aquarius, of wisdom and truth, we will no longer be able to sneak past urgent matters as we have done pastly.

To each his soul star

How can we inform ourselves through water? One way is to study our water crystal photographs. As I mentioned, at the Atelier für Kunst und Mystic, Ernst F. Braun and Sarah Steinmann photograph frozen water droplets. It is a process that only a few intuitive people can master. Since microscope photography is an expensive business, the world is not likely to see an abundance of it. You may want to give yourself a gift with the soul stars of your treasure, your children, pets, or plants. You can make your own water crystal photo book with these originals hang them as posters, on the wall. If it is a gift and must remain a secret, you can send a photo of the persons or animals involved to the Swiss artists. The traditional variant is: to get a 30 ml glass bottle with a plastic cap from the drugstore or pharmacy and fill it with distilled H_2O.

It would be best to inform the neutral wet as follows: First, you can label the lids 1, 2, and 3 or A, B, and C if you want more than one soul star. For example, your husband would be number 1, the oldest child 2, the youngest 3, the dog 4, etc. Put the bottles in the respective beds of the children who can't write their names yet. Make sure they are tightly sealed. If the children can smoothly write their name themselves, this will suffice. To generate a soul star for your pets, you can place the bottles in popular sleeping spots. A few hours should suffice.

Testing group dynamics

Are you unclear about staying loyal to a choir, or sports club, at a party or about saying goodbye? You could consult the soul stars. Take the small glass to the event. Ask the good souls who have passed on to scan the dynamic vibrations of the group and transfer them to the water. They would probably do it unsolicited. What could be more fun for them than to surprise us with their assessment while looking at the water crystals? In that way, perhaps they would succeed in bringing to their senses the lords and ladies of creation who like to sneak past the supernatural. And that is what is most important for those who have gone home.

Similarly, we could let the soul stars have their say when deciding whether to join a residential community. Perhaps the spiritual world would also be inclined to help with marriage counseling. We place the vial in the center of the family or group circle and ask people to turn to the water souls with their questions. I would interpret predominantly beautiful crystals as "yes." If there were mostly dark images with no crystalline structures, it would be a "no." With little psychic insight we can discover the reasons for the respective decisions in the water crystal pictures.

Creating soul stars by Ernst F. Braun and Sarah Steinmann

When a bottle of distilled H2O arrives at the studio, the 22 drops can be taken out immediately and frozen. So far, the artists have done well with the symbolic master number 22. When a bill with the signature arrives, they wrap it

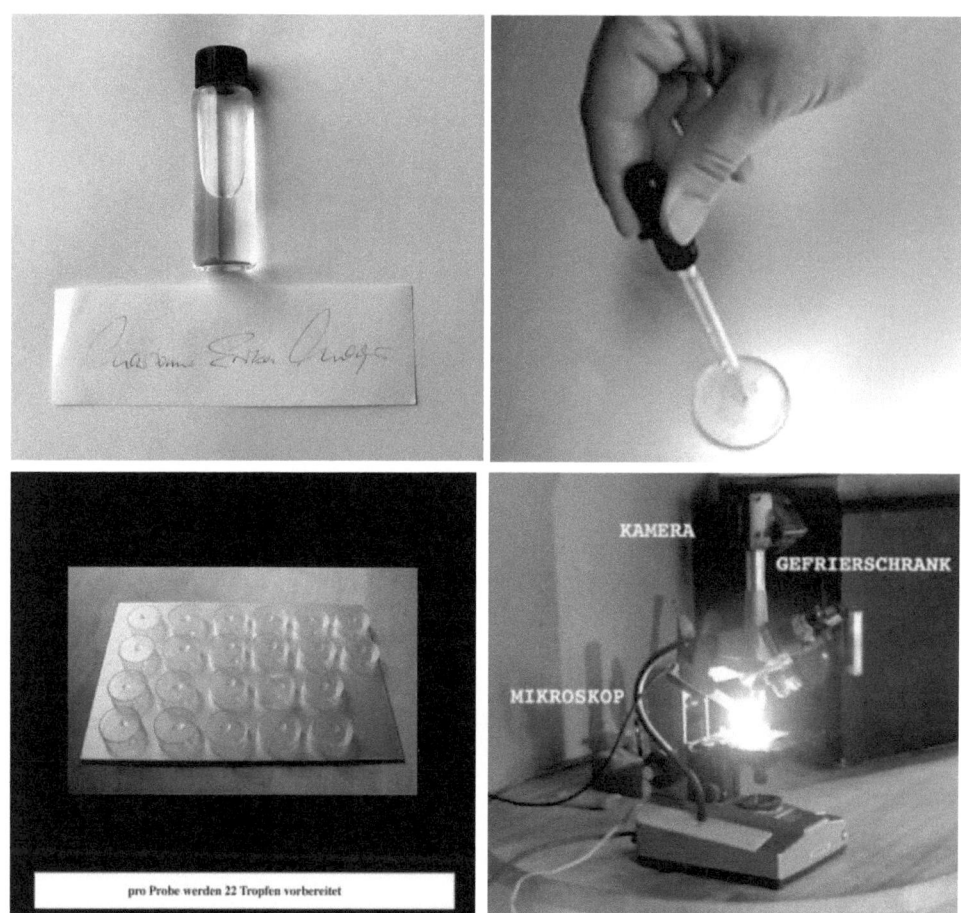

pro Probe werden 22 Tropfen vorbereitet

around a glass of purified water and leave it for about a day. They also place a bottle of distilled H2O on a photograph for about the same time. Then, Ernst Braun or Sarah Steinmann take 22 drops with the pipette and freeze them individually in Petri dishes at -30° for several hours.

Finally, the artists photograph the individual ice lumps under the microscope. Photographers must wait for the right moment. Shapes are not visible on each drop. As a rule, 8 WCP succeed. They select those with visible structures and optimize them regarding illumination and color. The shapes remain the same. Sometimes the photos tell whole stories. For me, they were milestones in my life. You will be surprised what messages the artists of this and the other world conjure up in and from the water. They are always unique. Only one artist can exactly recreate the water crystals. But also art or hobby painters can be inspired by crystals. The most beautiful picture, enlarged or painted, is an original gift. Is there anything more unique than your soul star?

IV. SOUL STARS - MILESTONES OF LIFE

Everything that exists seems to leave an imprint, an energetic structure, in the water. The Swiss water artists, inspired by Goethe's poem "Song of the Spirits over the Water", called it our energetic structure.

When Ernst Braun sent me my 15 soul stars, I only thought they were beautiful. But after looking at them several times, it occurred to me that most of the crystals represented milestones in my life: starting with the crystal I first called fertilization, despite Patentex prophylaxis. But later, it occurred to me that it may mark my prenatal trauma and forceps birth. I was three weeks overdue. See the previous page.

A happy tone and benevolent intentions form beautiful crystals. They seem to enjoy the blessing of the other world, for the astral artists painted harmonious, bright pictures when it comes to pleasant or neutral things, as in the keyhole, the dog picture, or the medical sports incident with the moon hopper.

I am best able to interpret the formations generated by my writing. Of the 15 images that emerged from the water with my signature, I recognize scenes from my life. I see my husband several times, an eye, and my star sign Sagittarius (see page 23). In the water crystal photo at the lower left, I still recognize my craftsmanship in renovating our house on the edge of the Santa Monica

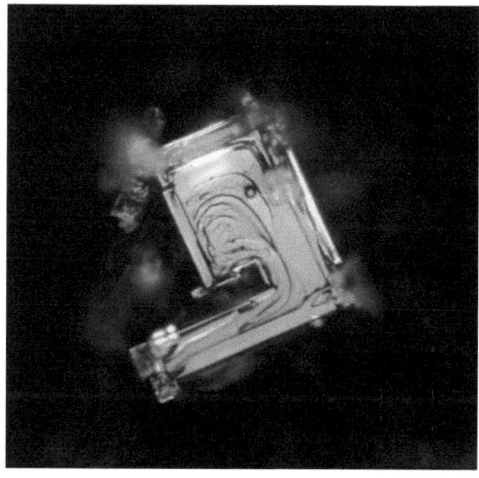

Mountains. The sphere representing the house is in an appropriate position about the mountains and the Pacific Ocean (ship). On the "eye" next to it, I first recognized my senile cataract, which Prof. Jäger had stung for me in Heidelberg when I was 13. Could it also represent an olive tree as a symbol of hope, peace, love, and living in harmony? The ohm sign could indicate good H_2O because the higher the resistance, the better the water. Perhaps it is also meant to confirm the statement of the water researcher Johann Tikale, who said that if you drank a lot of good water and bathed in it, you would not have gotten cataracts. Here you can gauge the number of possible interpretations!

As already mentioned, after studying my soul stars, I thought that beings from another world influenced the water. Among other things, they seem to transfer information to H_2O through the vibrations of writing. However, a secret experiment with Mrs. Steinmann, in which we asked about the whereabouts of a well-known person, suggests that names written with a computer can also give accurate information about persons.

The keyhole crystal symbolizes the feminine and the one next to it symbolizes the mourning for my dog. In the water crystal photo on page 42, which I interpret as fertilization despite intravaginal contraception with Patentex, the distinct structure is put into perspective by vague fragments. The bit of prenatal trauma also buzzed through my gray cells. But the soul star could also represent my forceps birth. I was three weeks overdue and had to be delivered.

That is perhaps why I am a person who likes to be challenged to do something. I always do my thing, read, write, paint, cook, or work in the garden. But otherwise, I like to be stimulated to do something. I traveled to Hamburg in the summer after Peter's transition because my friend Barbara Simonsohn invited me. I corrected a book for her as a thank you. Subsequently she got me a job as an editorial assistant. Financially I don't necessarily need it, because I am a frugal person and life in Portugal is considerably more affordable than in Germany. But I always wanted to be paid for reading whorsewhile health books and guides. But after proofreading the book "The Golden Path," I think I was led to Richard Rudd's work to learn more about the 64 gene keys. Because immediately after turning it in, I ordered the 728-page book "The 64 Gene Keys: Opening the Hidden Higher Destiny in Our DNA." Since then, there has been no work order. So I see my job as studying/being aware of the gene keys. See p. 104.

I interpreted the dog water crystal photo on the previous page as my love of animals and trees in my first book. Because of the raised ears, it resembles our Moroccan bitch. Looking at the WCP today, the brilliant-studded teardrop shape catches my eye, and I think of my tears when the French policeman gave me the collar of our run-over bitch. Sandy was born on the beach near Agadir on my birthday 1998, two months after my father's passing. The latter had not missed a single program of "Herrchen gesucht". So gladly, he would have had a dog. But the circumstances were not in his favor: the guests of the boarding house and the son working at night. For two years, Sandy delighted us with a course in dog love until she was run over near Geneva, a few hundred meters from Sir Peter Ustinov's final resting place. The day before, Sandy had said goodbye to my mother in a different way than usual by rubbing her head and nuzzling her several times. A year and a half earlier, I had dreamed that a French policeman handed me the red collar. I advised my mother not to get so emotionally attached to Sandy, as she would probably not live much beyond two years. It was two years and 24 days.

Again such a dream of truth. We all have prophetic dreams now and then, but most of us forget the night visions. Occasionally, something seems familiar: They register it as déjà vu. The program Galileo Mystery from October 24, 2008, was about the proof of prophetic dreams. It documented the case of the

Briton Chris Robinson during a scientific experiment by the US-American psychologist Dr. Gary Schwarz in the late summer of 2001. One of the dreams became a cruel reality shortly afterward:

Robinson saw airplanes flying into skyscrapers. A few days later came September 11. I also dreamed about the collapse of the WTC towers and the accident of our friend Marita, who died in her car only one hour before. I said to Peter the morning after the dream: "I hope that was just a movie, but it seemed like a report. I saw planes flying into the World Trade Center on TV. Both towers were on fire. They just collapsed like that. And afterward, I dreamt that Marita crashed into a truck."

It's certainly no proof for third parties, but anyone who deals with people who often have true dreams knows there is such a thing. The only reason it's so little research done is that there is little money to be made from it. And I have never been able to prevent any of my dream accidents because of the warning. Once I didn't get on a plane that didn't reach its destination because of considerable damage. At that time, apart from my mother and Peter, I had more than three hundred witnesses who witnessed the consequences of my prophetic dream. Robinson saw planes flying into skyscrapers.

Moonhopper, operations and High Priestess

In the following photo, which looks like a framed wedding picture, I thought at first: Those living in higher dimensions must know that Peter is considerably larger than me.

But later, I discovered the moon hopper below me. The WCP showed a scene some years ago: My husband helped me onto the plastic ring of the bouncy ball, which I tried for the first time. Indeed, standing on it, we were almost the same height. You may now ask: What kind of a landmark is that supposed to be? But for me, this piece of sports equipment was valuable. Because of it, I managed to solve my back problems. But maybe, a small trampoline is less accident-prone and not so easily destroyed.

The water crystal photos that do not reflect positive events look different. The following two WPCs required long work, but I cracked the code. They represent unnecessary operations. The first is particularly grim and low-frequency. It shows the removal of my appendix, which probably wasn't even inflamed.

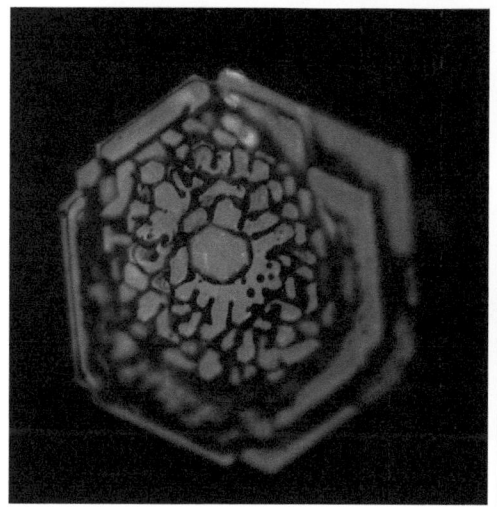

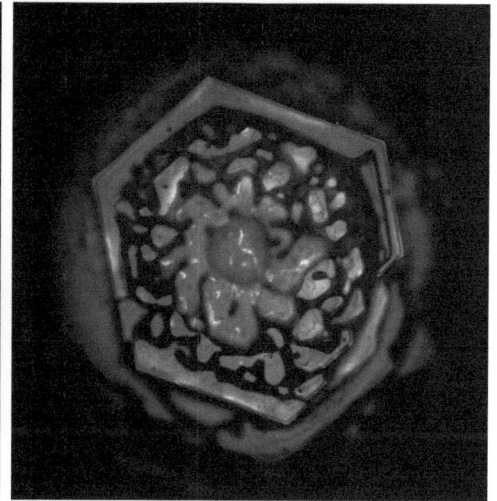

However, I did have post-operative inflammation. Without the breast enlargement, which the soul painters have depicted very clearly in the middle of this not-so-low-frequency WCP, I would possibly never have come up with the appendectomy. The appendix, as well as the tonsils, are organs of the immune system. If there is no life-threatening urgency, they should not be removed but treated with anti-inflammatory medications.

A friend recognized a skull with a crowning crystal bear in the following photo. Her interpretation: You will playfully enjoy life until your death - an elegant euphemism for a child's head. I see a kneeling praying woman and a chimera: saint and beast all united in man.

Mr. Braun made a postcard from the WCP and called it "High Priestess". He feels it is the perfect image for the book. He also saw a praying woman in a kneeling posture. I think the photo is mystical in any case. And mysticism, or better mediation between this world and the other world, it is. And it is also a theme in my life.

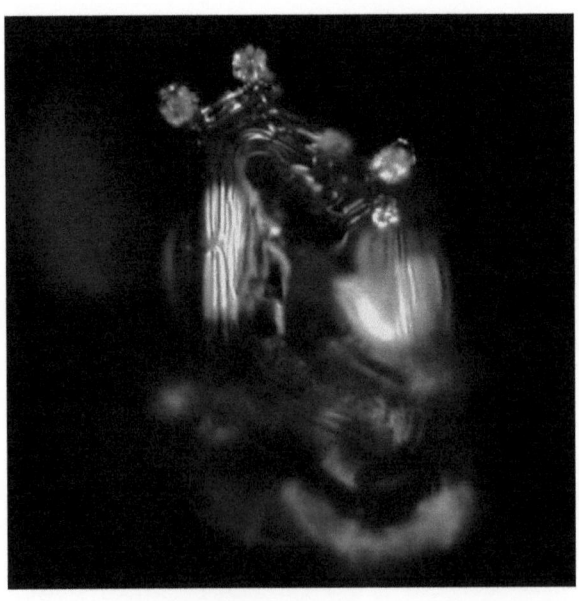

Wasserkristalle
nach M. Emoto fotografiert von

Ernst F. Braun
Gauggleren 2
CH-3664 Burgistein

+41 79 354 52 17
www.wasserkristall.ch
ernst_braun@bluewin.ch

SEELENSTERN

von Marianne Erika Meyer

DIE HOHEPRIESTERIN

Atelier für

KUNSTund Mystic

In this context, it occurs to me that some years ago, Ernst Braun emailed me the following microscopically photographed frozen drop of water with the request for interpretation. The artist took the water from an old churches well. I recognized a man and a woman intertwined in the bulging ring. The chin, mustache, and facial features reminded me of my husband! I still come to mind Odin, the God of war and death, probably because vinous Peter sometimes began to talk from Odin and swords.

Odin is also often depicted with long hair and horns. The WCP could also symbolize the Unio Mystica, the Holy Wedding, the becoming one with God, the highest aspiration of the mystics. This goal reaches when the spiritual disciple has attained the level of cognition of intuition.

https://anthrowiki.at/Unio_Mystica

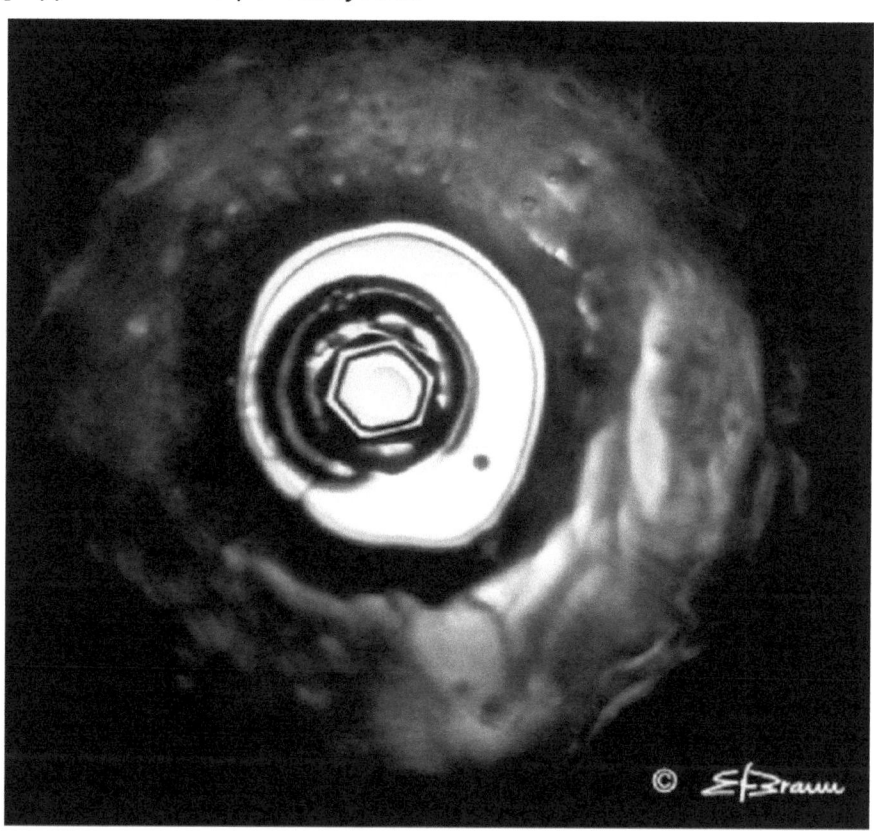

In any case, the rings you can see and a piece of braid indicate the bond. The plaiting is also a symbol of love, as two strands are tied together to form a braid. The fact that many weddings are celebrated in this church also speaks for love and bonding.

The photo below shows a staggered, broken crystal, similar to Emoto's, created by H_2O, sounding like the Elvis song Heart Break Hotel. I recognize elements that remind me of a difficult time in our lives in California: the moon symbolizing change and transition, a broken heart, and a gun stands for aggression and danger.

Peter had quit smoking and was compensating for nicotine withdrawal with vodka. At this time, he was about to going crazy. The cut-out from the crystal represents his silhouette. We almost got separated. Peter had started destroying the house. If I hadn't talked down to the officers, they would have shot Peter. At least that's what they told me.

Unfortunately, Peter has hidden his head under the baseball cap in this silhouette, or else, you could see how exactly the head fits into the outline of the tear-off.

Stars of the feline soul

Mr. Braun placed a vial filled with distilled water on the photo of tomcat Max for a while. Before energizing via pic or handwriting, H2O is very rarely able to create crystalline or hexagonal shapes on frozen drops.

The photographer's comment on this experiment: it seems to be a very spiritual, cute, and happy tomcat. You can read below how right E. Braun is. The content of the below crystal shows Max's favorite game.

In the USA, golf is a popular sport. We also practiced it. On the light-colored carpet in the room with the stone fireplace, we used the putter to try to get the golf ball into a black device, that then automatically returned the ball. Max liked to dash in between, eager to catch the ball.

Years ago, I only saw the oversized device with the white ball. Today I see photographically clearly on the left within the halo of rays looking from above the bald Peter in his leather vest looking to the southwest. The figure in between him and the golf ball looks like a Parcheesi piece, same as on an aerial photograph representing the young tomcat. Max also enjoyed playing in the hole on the lawn. At first, I thought the little WCP on the left was his joy in playing. Today I think the dot with the circle also symbolizes the divine and the soul power. As a so-called sun sign, it reflects us the "law of reflection and self-knowledge".

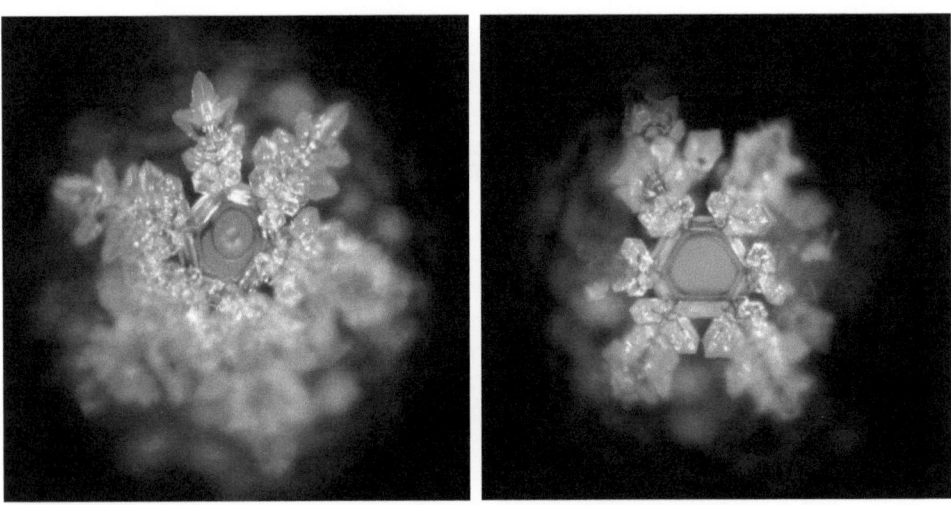

Max would have deserved the Nobel Peace Prize more than many a biped, as you can also read in "Family Code". He had managed to tame the rudest snot of white-booted gray fur. Sebastian, the neglected cat of the brain surgeon in our then-Californian neighborhood, had made life hell not only for his fellow cats. So long, that is, until I rescued the placid feline from the North Hollywood Animal Shelter.

At some point, Sebastian joined our two male cats and the white stray who often emptied a bowl at our house. Everyone seemed to respect the new territorial guru, whose black coat was decorated with a reverend accent and a touch of brown streaks that looked like a painter's brush had wiped on him. Max, who did not engage in any squabbling, exuded the dignity of a sage. Shortly before his death, he had come to me, and his demeanor had given me, as the only one of our animals, the opportunity to accompany him until his last breath. Max was a soul of a tomcat. He never had his claws out. He was more affectionate than all the other nearly twenty velvet paw creatures we were allowed to fill the bowls of in our 44-year life together. Two or three WCPs with heart shapes testify to this.

Mr. Braun took a few more photos than usual of Max. The one below, depicting a hexagon, represents, in my opinion, an accident witnessed by Max,

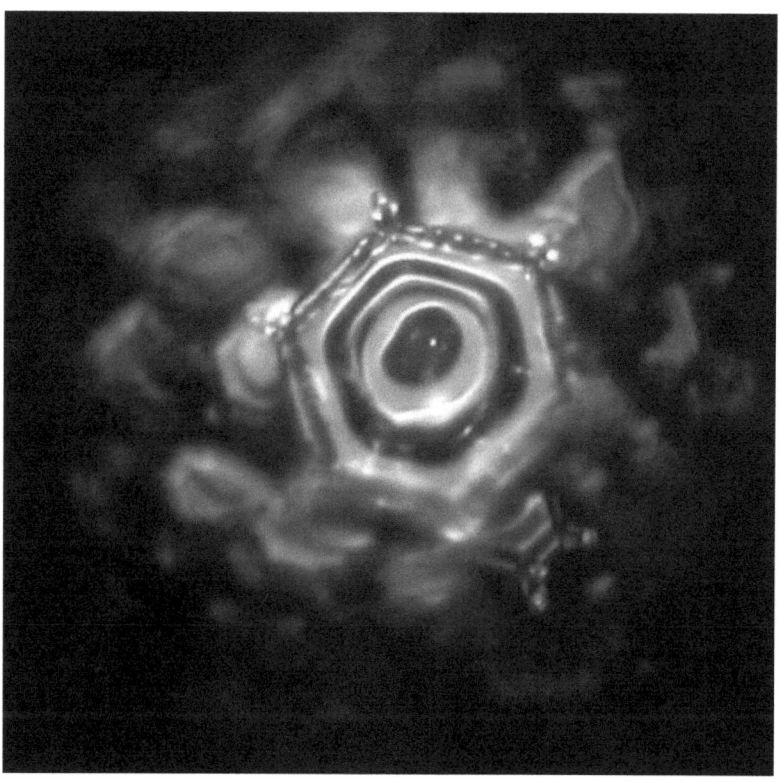

that led to the death of his con-specific Micky. The WCP showing my husband's accident (p. 64) has similar shading and texture. I think these shattered formations always show accidents, and if they also have a black circle with a white dot, as was the case with a WCP of a deceased friend, it is a fatal incident.

The split crystal below suggests the dire situation of Max in the winter of 2007/2008: He was missing for five days and arrived weakened and ulcerating from all holes. Max was probably locked in the storeroom or cellar of a neighbor's house: separated from us. The caricature of the man below left with glasses and parting also fits the neighbor who was away for a few days. The cat, right of the head, is better seen with a magnifying glass. Max never fully recovered.

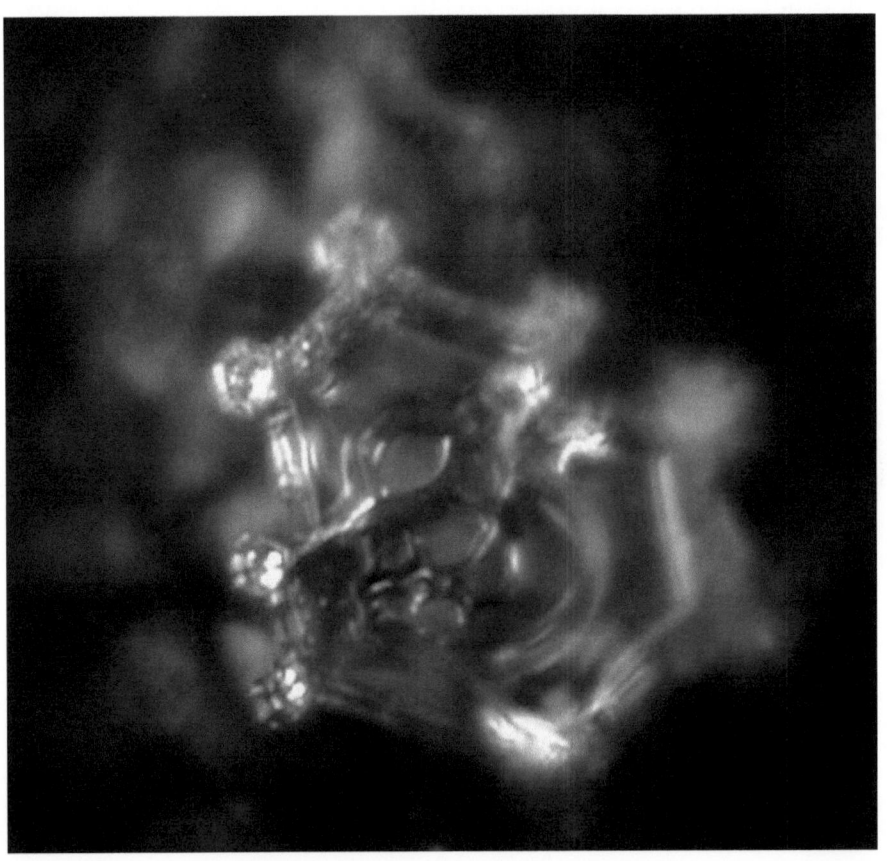

Can water crystal photos replace the crystal ball?

Perhaps you will find the answer to this question on the following pages. Or, as I said, you can have your soul stars taken. You could add a specific question to your signature. The advantage over the crystal ball is that you have all the time in the world when looking at the water crystal photos. You can consult mediumistic people or ask your soul self. See the chapter "Unfolding the inner guidance" for more information. A tip: Paint the water crystal photos of your choice with watercolor, oil, or acrylic. Painting is relaxing, and in a relaxed state, we usually have the best inspirations.

Birth trauma and another emotional shock

Since I made no bones about it and told Mr. Braun what I believed to read from the crystals, he e-mailed me four water crystal photos, which he photographed likewise in imitation of the procedure developed by Masaru Emoto. He hoped I would come up with something to go with his photos. Of course, once again, I was worried about not being good enough, not recognizing the right thing, etc., just the usual heart palpitations that probably most of us have in testing situations.

The Swiss researcher was born two months premature. As a child born in seven months, he suffered birth trauma. Mr. Braun wrote "shock at birth" on a slip and put dissolution symbols above it. He put a glass of distilled H2O on the paper and drank the informed wet later. In the process, it shook him up. After several days, he realized that something had gone away. He wrapped the writing around a vial of distilled water.

The transfer method to the water was similar to the creation of the soul stars.

After three days, Mr. Braun photographed the frozen water droplets. By e-mail, he asked me: "How did you perceive the photos of the test with the trauma? Do you see in it a possibility of an "information transmission"?

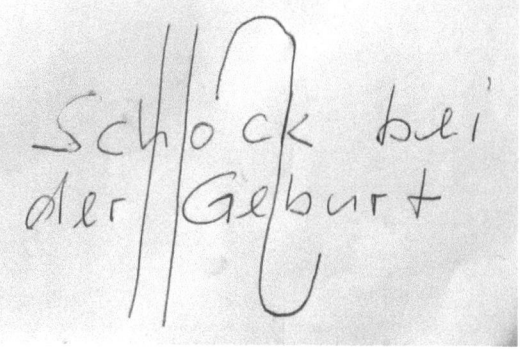

I looked at the four photos one after the other and wrote back: "To the 1st photo "joyful expectation/openness" comes to my mind. To the 2nd "break in the relationship" (to the father?). To the right above the break, I recognize an unhappy heart. Looking at the 3rd photo took a long time. It is also different in shape, something missing. It is something mechanical. 4. the calm after the storm. Everything is good again.

Mr. Braun then wrote back: "Hey, that's extremely interesting! And it's true. Yikes ..."

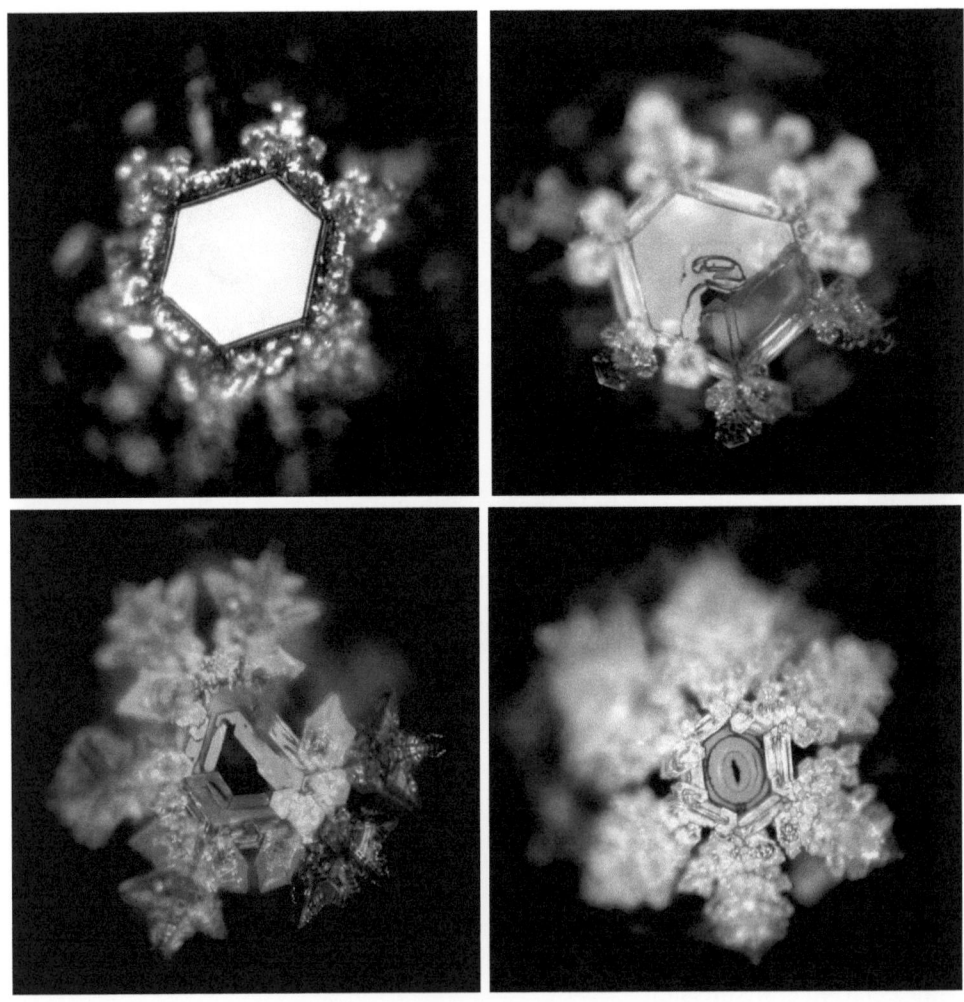

Although the Swiss prefer to photograph soul stars, Mr. Braun thought I could "read the stars" for them. I was immediately afraid of failing. The artist said: "We all have these fears. Some people face up to them. Others cover them up with raspberry sauce or something else. Who cares?

Well, I'm thinking of such a delightful experience at the end of a three-month seminar on the development of psychic abilities. A friend had urged me to participate. A half-Indian with a quarter of German and I were the best soothsayer. But when the leader, Taryn Krivé, invited 50 people to join us for a public demonstration, I almost wet my pants. Though, fear would not be an issue in the quiet of my own home. I also enjoy painting water crystals from time to time. A beneficial side effect: It is enormously calming and sparks the joy of experimentation, ingenuity, and creative design.

Prophecies through photos of water crystals

When I pictured the following crystal in a relaxed state while painting, I found that the Boomerang/Boot crystal was a prophecy, a message for me: one that heralded a sad event. The same is true for the water crystal photos I named *stone face* and *caught up in karma.*

Cocoon and stone face: signs of future depression

Looking at this soul star, I first thought of the message of an acquaintance who had passed away. For he had died in a prison cell. Almost everything fit: the cocoon in the upper part of the crystal, the person in a relaxed fetal position. The boomerang in front of the head and chest area also seemed to indicate: Everything we do to another falls back on us. The only disturbing thing was the thick knee joint: the acquaintance was strikingly delicate. A few weeks later, while painting, I realized this WCP was a prophecy: The bent creature in the cocoon can only represent my mother because of the beefy knees, and in the meantime, she withdrew completely into her snail shell. The pliers symbolize a predicament from which it is difficult to free oneself. My mother said she didn't want to deliver any more Christmas packages for the AWO. Shortly after, she caused a slight car accident and said, I have the receipt for my decision. Now I don't need a car anymore either.

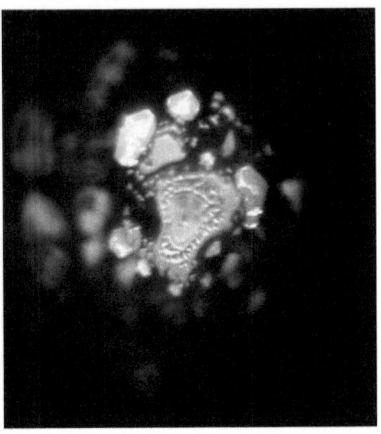

As my mother stirred in the remnants of her emotional low, I took her in. Peter did his rounds again as a test driver at the Nürburgring so that I could take care of her. Seizures soon followed, triggered by the wrong medication with a

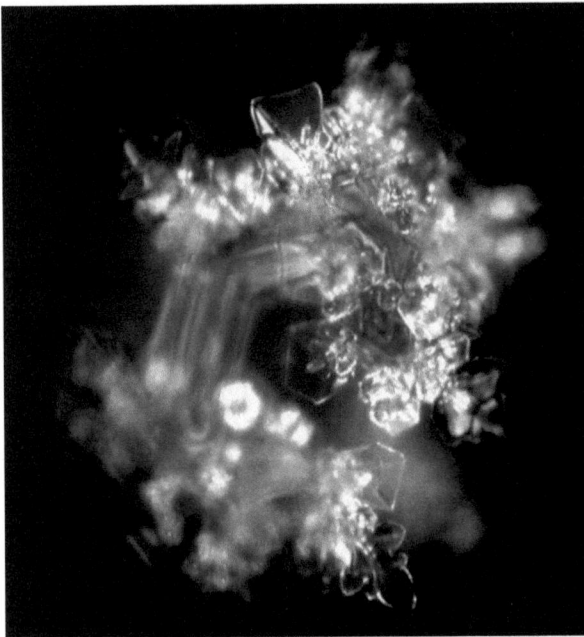

Until about 200 years ago, they used this instrument of torture to find out the truth. In dream interpretation, boots with a high shaft announce an arduous walk.

And what does the boomerang mean? Could her daughter-in-law's loose mouth have had a similar effect on my mother as her own sharp tongue had on her mother-in-law at the time? The latter also withdrew when she could no longer play a respectable role.

drug for dementia: sometimes manically cheerful, sometimes grumpily me-chanically driven, she talked crazy things and was afraid of torture. Whether the latter has to do with the boot in the WCP? They say: don't talk such a boot. Or does it stand for the Spanish boot?

Grandma Maria wandered the whole day over the meadow or sat in the car and looked over Michelstadt. Twenty years earlier, she was always there for us. She had nursed and cared for me like a chambermaid. Then, she was washed and diapered by her son. When I came home from my study at Frankfurt university, my parents hired me as a granny sitter. But on that day, Grandma's usual senility was blown away. I asked her to make me a sand-wich, just like in the old days. She rushed into the kitchen and made it for me. We browsed and talked and behaved as we always had. What if I had taken her with me to Frankfurt?

In order to prepare for (un)-retirement, it would make sense for people over 55 to form groups in communities and meet regularly with supervisors trained in gerontology. It could prevent many depression and retirement shock. Wouldn't it be wonderful if there were a school subject where we could learn to build relationships through improvisation or impromptu ac-tions? We would develop tolerance and respect towards all people: partners, parents, and children. And prepared for the respective stages of life, we could better avoid problems.

My husband Peter said my mother's biggest mistake was giving up her car and independence after a minor accident. Because of her heart disease, she had difficulty walking up the hill to the house. She was therefore, less flexible without a vehicle to maintain her social contacts and hobbies. More and more often, my mother stared at me inattentively out of eyes full of sorrow. Grief for her husband, her freedom, sadness, and fears seemed to eat away at her soul. Since she was taking a lot of medication, this could be another reason for her melancholy. After all, many chemical drugs can cause depression. My mother's face actually looked petrified a few months later.

Is water sovereign or the canvas of spiritual painters?

Water is sovereign and has its own will. Often it shows us forms and messages which do not correspond to our ideas. We, as the photographer, cannot contribute much to it and therefore cannot give you a guarantee for beautiful stars.

That is how Ernst F. Braun sees it. By this, he means: The water shows what it wants to show us. The artist's words remind me of the clairvoyant with her crystal ball. She, too, cannot guarantee that the client will like what she shows. But the advantage of the water crystal photos is obvious: We can see a picture. Even if the fortune teller allowed us to look at the crystal ball, we would probably not see anything. Tense expectation and stage fright would rob us of calm and perspective. Even at home in peace, I could only enjoy the beautiful pictures at first glance. I discovered episodes, events, and turning points only by looking closely.

Until a few years ago, I also thought that water was sovereign. The title of my book Wunderwesen Wasser bears witness to this. But E. Braun's work gave me the idea that the dead want to communicate with us using water, crystal ball, tea set, etc. To confirm this assumption, in another experiment, I added to my name the question of whether my deceased father and two recently deceased acquaintances have something to communicate to us.

Following, I interpret the pictures that tell me something. But first, an exhilarating experience: I went with my husband to the post office to send the note with the question to the deceased. In my mind, I was with my father and asked him to give me a clear sign. On the way back, I glanced at an advertising poster with sausage varieties. Although I usually avoid sausages, it drove me to the store where the kind Russian shopowner usually sold me Siberian cranberries:

An inner urge makes me point to a chicken salami and two more sausages. With a filled plastic bag I leave the store under Peter's equally astonished and delighted gaze. After climbing the Kisselberg, we sit on the fountain edge to rest. Suddenly I am overcome by a hellish ravenous appetite. I say, let's try the salami. Throwing all hygienic concerns overboard, Peter sabers away at the salami with the key.

I think: Hopefully, no one comes by thinking of a reader of my books whom I often meet. He walks around the town almost every day. A fraction of a second later, he rushes past us. I snort: What's going on today? Later, in a quiet minute, the scales fell from my eyes: hadn't I asked my father for a clear sign? But I thought of one concerning the water crystal photos. Had my old man arranged all this so amusingly? First transferred his desire for sausages to me for a couple of hours and then sent the health-conscious man by at the very moment I thought of him. Thanks, Pa, for your imaginative cooperation!

Searching for the written work

When I opened the file with the water crystal photos attached to the e-mail, the first thing that beamed at me was the purest soul image. Again, I overcame with the same feeling of happiness that I had when my late father used me as a medium. He had doubted that we live on after death. I used to say: you will ex-perience it, then give me a sign. And what a sign of his existence he gave me: the funeral service with chorals and Bible quotations he let resound in me in advance, e. g. "I pray to the power of love" and "Behold I am with you always ...". Each morning, I woke up with a different verse. I was extra alert on the first day. In the evening, I thought about what the reason leading to death might have been. In the morning, I heard the International ringing in me. I asked my mother if she had an explanation for it. She knew immediately: my father was still awake when the election night ended at the end of September 1998. In the end, comrades usually sing, "Peoples hear the signals ...". Was the hoot that his weak heart made for joy possibly too powerful?

After inscribing the note, I thought of the novel my father wrote in the early 1950s. I wondered where he had kept it. The crystal interior of the WCP looks like a house. An eye on the roof seems to be on a rectangular structure in the long corner. It borders a spot that looks like a crack in the ceiling. I went to the attic with my mother. She pointed to a strip of tinfoil placed over the insulation material and said: It looks like the "crack" in the roof. I followed the eye and walked in a stooped pose toward a shelf at the far back. Yes, exclaimed my mother, that's where he kept his paperwork. In a folder, I found manuscripts from 1951. My father must have sent them to an agency because it offered him: For 12.50 marks, we send fifty copies to various publishers. I read the story "So I became a writer" right away. I'll gladly reveal the beginning to you

since, in the case of the usual author's hourly wage, measured against the fees, the statement is still valid after 60 years. Here is my father's text published posthumously: combined with the wish that the currently much-discussed citizen's income may soon improve the situation of beleaguered cultural creatives:

He was not skilled at working on the drill press. Only extreme necessity would have led him to apply for a job at the factory. Day after day, he put his metal blades into the template. And day after day, he came to me to have his broken drill bits resharpened or replaced. That's how we got to know each other. He had never achieved the desired goal. I soon realized that he was used to other work. Once I approached him:

"Tell me, colleague, this way of earning money doesn't appeal to you very much either. What is your profession?"

Aware of his grand mission, he explained to me majestically:"Writer!"

"So, why do you have to earn your dough as an unskilled worker?"

"Well, the poet and thinker have never counted for much in Germany. With us, the genius can starve if he wants to!"

We used to play skat more often. My father usually said: He who writes stays. Though in a different context, we both stay now. You may now think I write because my father would have liked to become a writer. But I look forward to writing. When I have done other necessary physical work, I prefer to rest by writing. I have been writing letters since I was a child. Reading and writing have always been my favorite pastimes.

Caught up with karma

Years ago, I dreamed of a friend standing at the front door with a black suit-case. When I have prophetic dreams, I remember them for the rest of my life. I took it as an indication of his imminent demise, for I saw him in black trousers and vest, a white shirt with ruffles and puffy sleeves.

My mother had a similar dream years ago. A few weeks after her friend showed up in her night vision with a black suit-case, he died. In G's case, the Grim Reaper took a little longer to come for him.

The clear chiseled half-crystal with the black man on the left seems to be a message from our friend: he moved away from the good life and turned his back on his family. He'd fallen into ruin in search of new fortune. The mistress exploited him even further than he instrumentalized the people around him.

Do we foresee our fleshly end?

The next soul star I interpret as Peter's car accident since he had broken his left shoulder joint in an accident in the test car. All the more so since I vaguely recognize the distinctive facial features of Michael Schumacher in the mirror.

But when I first saw the WCP, I thought it would show Matze's accident. Our neighbor's classmate must have anticipated his demise. He began avoiding things that might bring about an early death. He gave up his motorcycle. Some-time before dawn, an oncoming driver suddenly braked because of a run-over animal. She lost control of the car and Matze his bloody young carnal life.

Many people seem to foresee their physical end. My father made a folder ev-ery year. On the last one, he wrote "end of Sep 98". He died on Oct 1, 1998.

Peter made more declarations of love to me in his last ten days than in the past ten years. He talked about our beautiful life together, our travels through the continents, and that we can draw from our memories.

Months before her fatal accident, a woman in black appeared at our friend in a black limousine. At our last meeting, Marita said goodbye very warmly.

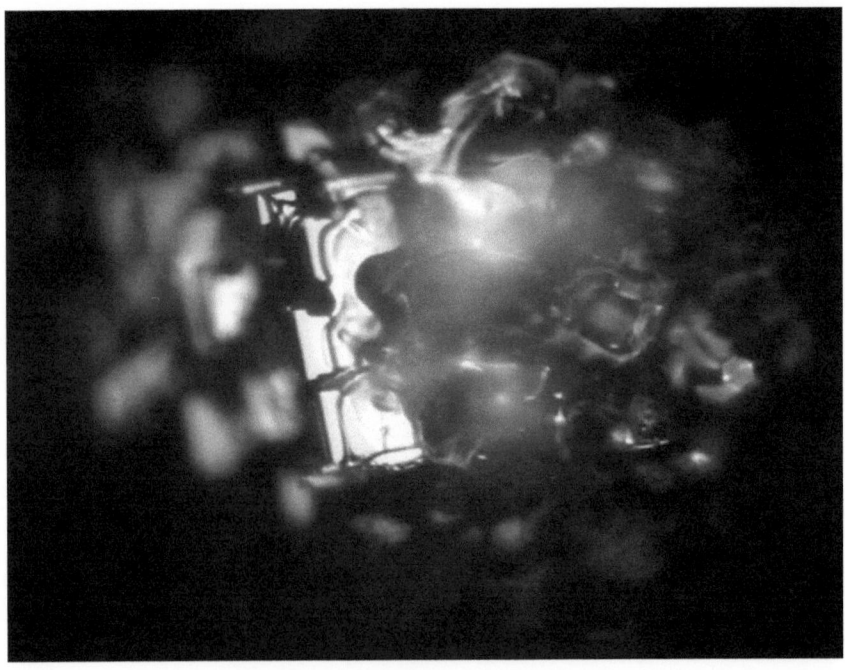

Leo, my goddaughter's husband, said before he died that he no longer had an guardian angel.

Fairy-tale scenes

During the following tests with neighbor children about twenty years ago, Ernst Braun put the slip of paper with the respective signature on a vial of distilled water to inform it. With Daniel's first soul star, which resembles a snowflake, I remembered his mother, who liked snow very much. His mother had left her bodily shell when she was 39 years old. You can see the number 39 in the lower part of the hexagon. Daniel's mother once told me that on her birthday, a snowflake fell, although it had not snowed on that December day. She interpreted this as a greeting from her mother.

Daniel's other soul star looks like an illustration of a fairy tale. A female sits on the bent back of a long-nosed man (a symbol of mockery or scorn) and looks at a figure reminiscent of Manneken Pis. Back then, I had interpreted it as a baby, but now the meaning of the figure standing in Brussels has become clear to me. To the left of it, I see a harlequin mask and, below, a duck's head. The harlequin symbolizes a figure of dual nature: trickster and healer, priest and devil, shaman and joker and artist (Wikipedia). That was indeed true of Daniel's father. He was a gifted osteopath who had studied at the University of Brussels (Manneken Pis!). The duck's head seems to symbolize the Lame Duck. In the USA, a lame duck is a politician incapable of acting, notably in domestic politics. That was also the case with Daniel's father, who had to submit to a temporary occupational ban and died during this time, separated from his family.

The dark animal below between the girl and Manneken Pis looks like a gorilla. The gorilla is considered erratic and headless. Daniel's mother said to this WCP only: I know the monkey down there.

As I said, I had these insights only years later. That's why it is so interesting to look at the soul stars again every five to ten years. Also, with the WCP of Max

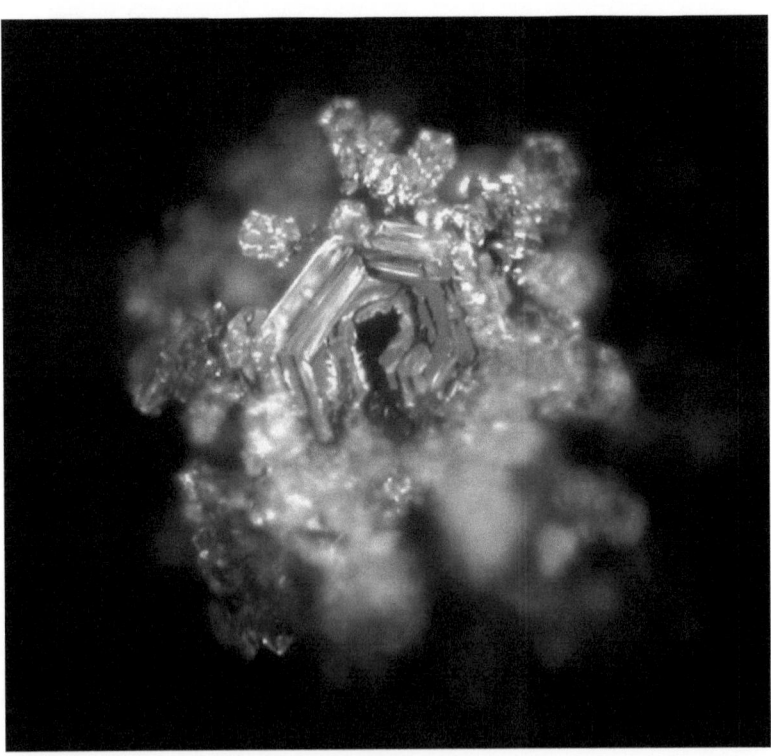

on page 51, I recognized my husband only about three years ago. Likewise, the funny little doll is a head replacement on my soul star, star representing my star sign Sagittarius, on page 23.

Who collects that many clovers?

Sometimes Daniel's mother would find several at a time on our lawn. Every time she climbed over the hunter's fence, her trained eyes would roam the greenery. When she lent me books, I often found whole bundles of dried four-leaf clovers. The WCP on the next page, which E. Braun thought was Daniel's designated soul star, clearly shows a four-leaf clover. Except for Daniel's mother, I don't know other people who are so persistent in looking for these lucky charms. That's why there was a shamrock for him twice.

The soul star of his sister below also shows a shamrock. Does she, rather than her mother, carry the fourth, much larger leaf as a burden on her back? Is this a matter of karmalogy? I think it is Daniel's mother's heavy fate despite the 4th shamrock.

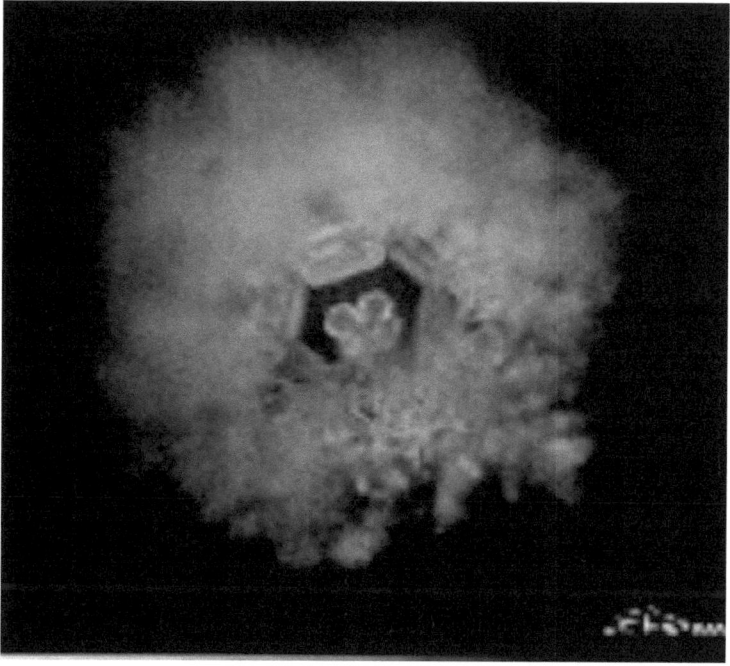

Pandora's box

Because of the green color and chromosome-like formations, I thought of Daniel's interest in biology and medical research when I saw WCP below. The first thing that came to mind was: Hopefully, it has nothing to do with genetic engineering.

Let's remember how once the majority of our people instinctively and unequivocally rejected genetic manipulation. After years of targeted brainwashing, has the public consciousness become numb to the initially rigorous rejection of life-threatening techniques? If, as Spiegel Online reported on Feb 28, 2018, Barbra Streisand had her dog cloned twice, who is to guarantee that other celebrities won't clone human pets in the future?

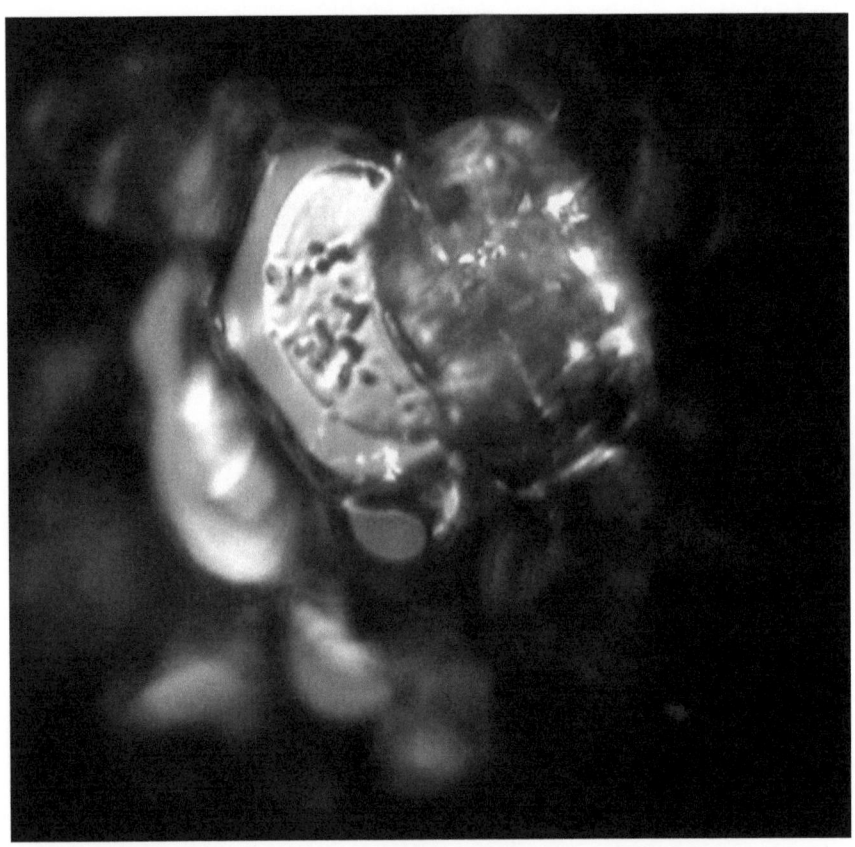

Is history repeating itself once again? Let's better ask that we can make the Frankensteins of the world aware of their dangerously confused work. Otherwise, it can happen that we must flee soon again from flying monsters and may admire lion-bodied human heads, not only stony in Egypt. Does everything have to repeat itself? Because of our bondage to institutions, we have only a vague awareness of right and wrong. Instead of relying on media, authorities, or sciences, we better listen to our inner voice and reflect on our original feelings towards a healthy life. We better actively counteract the massive potential danger to avert grander damage. Of course, we can also use our power as consumers!

Daniel, a teenager at the time, is dealing with bones today, just like his blessed father did many years ago. He has become a dentist. This WCP looks similar to those indicating accidents ... or pain? Both can apply to this profession. Daniels sister's WCP I named: hanging in the ropes.

V. USING THE POWER OF THE UNIVERSE

Analogous to the microcosm of man, the macrocosm of the universe works. "As in heaven, so on earth," says the Bible. What resonates above resonates below. Whatever we miss from the microcosm man, we find in the macrocosm universe. As explained above, homeopaths potentize active substances to imbue the sick with this missing information. For this purpose, it is necessary to detach the active substances of plants, minerals, or animals from their bodily manifestation. Alternative medicine practitioners couple the information freed from its material binding to suitable information carriers (aqua marina, alcohol, lactose to pass it on. The more they shake, the more the plant essence is freed from material captivity, and the more powerfully the information can unfold in non-material space.

Fields of consciousness - bridges to the beyond

We are all connected through the universal field of consciousness. How this works, I make it plain for you with an example. One evening before Pentecost about fourteen years ago, I called my mother and said: We are going to the townlet now. She had already hiked but asked about our usual route: Gemüsetürke - Rathaus - Lindenplatz. When we were down the hill, Peter said, let's go to the big square on the main road. At Whitsun, the people from Michelstadt still celebrate the bee market here since my mother, as a city councilor, voted against its abolition many years ago. Foreigners call the citizen of Michelstadt "bees" because a bee once saved the town by sitting on the nose of the tower guard, who had fallen asleep.

As we turned the corner to the fairground, I saw my mother approaching at a stately pace. She said, "Actually, I wanted to go to the town hall. But all of a sudden, I was drawn in this direction." We are, after all, connected to our loved ones in the afterlife through numerous dimensional fields. Could my father, as he did in the fall of 1998 when he had his funeral service with hymns and biblical quotations - "I pray to the power of love" and "Behold, I am with you always ..." - have sounded in me, telepathically orchestrated the encounter? Can pets also find their home thousands of kilometers away in this way? Animals have souls like us. Only so the phenomenon makes sense: Animal-loving deceased or dog souls or velvet paw beings in the other world help their conspecifics in the flesh, just as our deceased ones lead us now and then on the right way.

Water and the resurrection of life

All that wetness in the 3-pound piece of meat called the brain begs the question: Who or what is thinking? Is or does H_2O reflect consciousness? In world religions it is often a sacred symbol for transmitting mysterious life forces. But the inquisitors in the Middle Ages seemed to sense an abysmal danger in the noble energy of sensitive people. Therefore, they extinguished those blessed too richly with holy water with fire. However, it would be a blessing for our planet if the ruthless militant rulers realized that they must expect to be bombed themselves in the next life. Also, if environmental sinners would know that they have to suffocate in the polluted environment in future lives or rapists and child molesters would be desecrated themselves or get in touch with perverted tormentors: An eye for an eye, a tooth for a tooth. Whether it is so maybe irrelevant here. It would be a way to escape the "after me, the deluge" mentality.

We are usually biased when we lack the discerning experience of others. But since my walk over glowing coals, I know: Everything is possible (Meyer 2016). We all can, whether by ourselves or through spiritual help, raise our vibrational frequency and perform so-called miracles.

Rebirth is no more miraculous to Voltaire than being born once. Many other famous men who made a name for themselves as philosophers, scientists, and artists dealt with the transmigration of the soul for purification. These included Socrates, Pythagoras, Aristotle, Cicero, Caesar, Michelangelo, Plato, Frederick the Great, Kant, Goethe, Fichte, Hegel, Schopenhauer, Wagner, Nietzsche, Schweitzer, Heine, Edison, Einstein, and of course, C.G. Jung. Early Christianity also believed in reincarnation, as did the Hindus and Buddhists for several centuries B.C. But a few hundred years after Christ's birth, church leaders came to the idea that reincarnation was less good for business because it involved self-responsibility and independence. Therefore, they rejected the re-embodiment of the soul in another body on the part of the church. But to save

Rebirth is no more miraculous to Voltaire than being born once. Many other famous men who made a name for themselves as philosophers, scientists, and artists dealt with the transmigration of the soul for purification. These included Socrates, Pythagoras, Aristotle, Cicero, Caesar, Michelangelo, Plato, Frederick the Great, Kant, Goethe, Fichte, Hegel, Schopenhauer, Wagner, Nietzsche, Schweitzer, Heine, Edison, Einstein, and of course, C.G. Jung. Early Christianity also believed in reincarnation, as did the Hindus and Buddhists for several centuries B.C. But a few hundred years after Christ's birth, church leaders came to the idea that reincarnation was less good for business because it involved self-responsibility and independence. Therefore, they rejected the re-embodiment of the soul in another body on the part of the church. But to save humanity and our planet, it would be opportune to reintroduce it today. Because, as said, if we would firmly count on having to live again in another body one day, we would surely deal more carefully with our environment.

Due to the many scientifically proven cases of reincarnation, we can hardly ignore several earth lives in other bodies. There is the worldwide known case of the Indian Shanti Devi: Her memories of previous earth lives proved to be exact. Such authorities as the psychoanalyst C.G. Jung, the physicist Oliver Lodge, the psychiatrist Morris Netherton, the parapsychologist Hans Bender, the internist John Björkhem have come to equally astonishing results in countless other cases. Dr. Björkhem alone collected 600 case studies: e. g. an English sports teacher speaks under hypnosis in an ancient Egyptian dialect, and an American woman speaks a 1000-year-old, almost forgotten oriental language. A man who never learned foreign languages writes in 28 languages under hypnosis (Netherton and Shiffrin 2005).

Throughout our lives, we change shape and lose more and more water. If we leave our body one day to continue to exist in another dimension, the soil takes up our wet again. Through the water cycle, we experience: Nothing passes away. Water has been coming from space in giant snowballs since time immemorial, combining with clouds and raining down to feed bodies of water. Or how would you interpret these photos from a NASA space probe in 1996? (The link below the picture will take you to another pic from May 1997.).

But how did all life on Earth begin? Who greened the planet? Just as humans want to green Mars today, it could have been greened by aliens in its day using fossil blue-green algae. We know that single-celled organisms use sunlight to split water molecules to produce their food from the surrounding gases. They process carbon dioxide into carbohydrates and nitrogen into amino acids and proteins. In the process, they release oxygen and create a life-friendly system for aerobes.

Cyanobacteria form a recycling system with humans and animals as they require oxygen and release carbon dioxide. They were probably also the manna used to feed the Israelites in the desert (Meyer, 2016).

I don't find the idea so far-fetched that people who vehemently dislike or are allergic to spirulina could be the rein-carnated Jews who supposedly wandered in the desert for 40 years. After 40 years of eating blue-green algae, one might have lost one's appetite. How about a regression for all those who can't tolerate spirulina?

Were they victims of an extra-terestial experiment? It could also explain the length of stay and the lion's "gold".

https://apod.nasa.gov/apod/ap970530.html

Vibrations and resonance - we are what we think

What do we know about the vibrations of the mind? They have a wavelength and are different from person to person: like the fingerprint. If we send out good vibrations, good things happen to us. Unhealthy vibrations attract mischief. If we are joyful and grateful, we invite good vibes in the sense of resonance. So we attract what we send out and receive what we give. Or: As we call into the forest, it echoes back.

When we nag and complain, we create even more reasons to complain. Although it helps to express one's opinion for better understanding, it would be highly detrimental to a good relationship if we caused the other person pain or a guilty conscience.

According to the resonance principle, we best strike the tone we want to hear. Or, as Kant puts it in his categorical imperative: Act only according to the maxim that you can make a general law. Many years ago, my mother said to me: "Your neck is already wrinkled. At that time, I only thought, why would she tell me that? Does she want me to feel bad? Later, when I saw us interacting in a past life after meditation, I realized the reason for her behavior. She was a beautiful concubine who teased me constantly, mainly because of my height. I would cut a ridiculous figure for a Roman legionnaire. At one point, she so enraged me that I cut off her breasts with one blow of my sword. I buried the weapon in the sand and took off. That has to do with the shadow frequency violence that I have in the 20th gene key of evolution and the 34th of the life work (see p. 107). In our mother-daughter life together, my mother unconsciously took revenge by giving me things I did not like. When I talked to her about this past life and told her that the only gift I had ever been enormously happy about was the wash leather trench coat with the balloon cap she had brought me from her vacation in Turkey, she said: Mike picked that one out. So in my case, I can explain my mother's behavior. I hurt her badly in a previous life. I found this out in a 3-month workshop to develop our psychic abilities. In the present life, she loved me, but unconsciously she often symbolically drew the sword. If I did not have the 60th siddhi in the hologenetic profile, for whom past and future exist in the now and I did not remember any past lives, insults would lead to the question, why does she keep hurting me? So thoughts and feelings create vibrations. We are what we think. If we believe God is all love and within us, this belief will shape our behavior. If we believe that our destiny is to suffer, we create suffering.

The following chapter shows how you can harmonize vibrations and shape your soul.

Making optimal decisions with vibrational harmony

We can consciously harmonize our vibrations: through breathing exercises and soul shaping. If we let ourselves guide by our soul, we follow the elemental will or the golden path. Then we live in harmony with creation and are in tune with the unconscious regulating or self-healing forces of soul energy. Then we recognize our driving forces and know how to implement them. We find our guidelines in life and follow them confidently, trusting our inner authority in our decisions. We develop a master plan that leads to more fulfillment and success.

How do we deal with problems? Let's breathe calmly and deeply, harmonizing the rhythm of breathing. We now direct the uninhibited vibrations, like the focused light vibrations of a burning lens, to the location of the disturbance. In this way, we challenge the striving of the unconscious control forces for vibrational harmony. That initiates the momentary optimum. Let us now look at a problem on our inner screen without taking it up: without brooding, let us immediately allow ourselves a pleasant thought. It doesn't matter whether we think of a happy past event or revel in the happiness expected in the future: It is crucial to concentrate on our feeling, on happy things and leave problems aside for the time being. Feeling good, we can deal with our difficulties free from fear, doubt, and disturbing thinking. So let us be lovely and praiseworthy, heartfelt and helpful, essential and valuable. We don't even need to have experienced it ourselves since we are all connected by soul energy. It is enough to admire individual people and rejoice in their successes. Or we look forward to the time after the problem is solved. So we sketch a picture in our soul, which serves as a template for shaping the soul energy. Let us turn our consciousness to the blissful because uplifted the soul will process the ballast.

We live carefreely, provided we can turn off our thoughts and satisfy or overcome our desires. The physician and wisdom teacher Dr. Nobuo Shioya, who lived to be 106 years old, leaves us with three simple rules for an optimal life: 1. look at everything positively. 2. do not nag. 3. do not forget gratitude. Looking at the WCP on p. 18, I would like to add one more rule or advice: Sometimes, it is better to part with partners before the horse's foot, which stinks of sulphur, stomps on them.

Are we able to program the inner being?

Yes! On a journey of discovery into the unconscious, we shape our vibrations. The soul field around us also resonates. In resonance with the All-Soul, we feel harmony.

The shaping of our soul field serves the fulfillment of our desires. In doing so, the soul establishes the proper connection to the other areas.
It works without our conscious intervention. After we have attuned ourselves to a sense of comfort, as mentioned above and feel the well-tuned field of our soul energy, we move it to the place of wish fulfillment. For example, if you want to take a trip around the globe, you'll probably want to figure out how to raise the money. But the soul programming looks different: The energy field of your soul only radiates that you will see the world. You are inwardly experiencing something that could and should indeed occur. We anchor or form a possible reality in our soul field in advance. Our soul takes over this pattern as reality, stores it, and slips into the new form given by us. Through soul programming, we also progress with other plans: for example, finding a job or the right partner. Thus we steer our life course in the direction of optimal coincidences. But we do not need to want anything in particular. We are filled with hopes and desires and strive to find the right path to our self-fulfillment. That succeeds if we merely live in joyful expectation and delight our fellow men with our talents. Because if we work with genuine joy according to our passion, that is already rewarding.

What can we learn from children?

The soul that sees beauty is a soul thought to be insane by the majority. How well do I understand these words of Goethe. As far as physical functions are concerned, we may have come close to the ideal of creation. But regarding the spiritual level, it would be high time to set out on the path to perfected form. Children can help us to stay on course, but also to break new ground sometimes. Their authenticity and impartiality can guide us. We need only pay attention to their behavior and words. Sometimes they tell us about their imaginary friends. My great-nephew Moritz told us about his experiences with a Christian when he was three to four years old. But there was no Christian in the kindergarten, the neighborhood or the circle of acquaintances. Only my father's uncle, killed in the Russian campaign, was named Christian. Two years ago, Jonas, Moritz's younger brother, began to talk about Simon. When asked who that was, he said, that is my brother; he died five years ago. A year later, I asked Jonas if he was still seeing Simon. Upon his answering in the affirmative, I asked again who that was. Now he said, that is my brother who died six years ago. My niece had lost a fetus at that time. That means even unborn children continue to develop in the higher dimensions and join their fleshly relatives. Is it possible that one day they will show us the way to the light? I am already looking forward to my children. I named one boy Jan Jasper and had seen him in a dream shortly after conception. He would be 36 years old today. I had these miscarriages probably because of all the x-rays I had to take in a transit doctor's office as a physician's assistant. My daughter-in-law, also exposed to x-rays as a physician's assistant at an orthopedic surgeon's office, had the same experiences.

In the late 1980s, a Phil Donahue show in the U.S. was about a child who had been declared clinically dead on the operating table. When the girl's soul returned to the body, she described having been in a lovely garden greeted by her brother and dog. The surgeon wondered, knowing that the girl was an only child. He spoke to the mother. She was surprised and delighted and said that she had given birth to a son before her daughter, but he had died shortly after birth. They had never mentioned this to the girl.

My mother said I had already spoken quite clearly about certain things at age two, but she did not understand them. In the past, grown-ups often ridiculed children. They told them not to fantasize like that. But today, many parents seem to push back wisdom and truth less. They are asking about the beings that join their children. More people are turning to the metaphysical. They learn from children to become more sensitive to truth and untruth.

We can all learn to overcome fear and develop self-esteem. Ernst F. Braun's water crystal photographs can help transform our fear into awe. When we understand their message, we will trust the cosmic forces of our souls.

Water - mediator between the worlds

If we come into contact with the forces of the cosmos, it can develop into an exciting and never-ending task. Wind, waves, vortices, water: What do we know at all about the laws of nature? Goethe's words mean: "The soul of man resembleth water: From heaven it cometh, to heaven it soareth. And then again to earth descendeth, changing ever." As I already mentioned, water can pour into any form without losing its essence. Be it solid, liquid, or gaseous, it conducts electric and subtle energies. We are electromagnetic beings and know from experience how it is with lightning and its discharges. Less known is that water also serves as a transmitter and receiver, i. e. mediator of messages. That can be seen not only in the mentioned works of Hahnemann, Emoto, or Ernst F. Braun but also in my experiences with water crystal photography and especially in the plausible interpretation of the crystal pictures. Our body water also receives messages. Our soul or consciousness is always there and dances for thousands of years like the changeable water in unique archetypal patterns through our varying bodies. At times, we find ourselves struggling with our shadows, while at other times, we feel a deep peace. Our lives, each of which we can view as waiting for death, resemble the flame of a candle flickering endlessly back and forth in the wind of duality, from fear to trust, from patience to impatience, and back again. See also the chapter What makes us unique?

Based on my dreams of past lives in watery environments, I imagine it this way: The mind is not only in the brain, but all levels of consciousness are in the membranes of all our cells, i. e. the skin, bones, and organs. So every single cell in the body is electromagnetically connected with each other and the universe. Via cellular water, every impulse within us transmits to the universe. Thus it is also possible to stimulate the cell memory and to let past lives pass in review. That is also proven thousands of times by psychiatrists during regressions.

VI. WATER TESTS WITH MY LATE HUSBAND

My husband's sudden death on Feb 11, 2017 was the most upsetting experi-ence in my 67-year-old life. We had finished packing our camper for the trip to Morocco. I was cleaning the house while Peter was working on the car. Sud-denly, I heard him let out a scream. When I got to the front door, he collapsed, and I tried to hold him down. Bubbles were coming out of his mouth, and his facial skin was cyanotic. It was immediately clear his wish to go to a higher lev-el of consciousness was being fulfilled. He had indirectly told me a few days earlier that he would not stay with me much longer in his usual form.

The story behind the tests and the book Sad News

On February 28, 2017, a psychic acquaintance called me. Isabel Bannier-Groß said she had just been sitting at her computer when suddenly a sepia-colored book cover appeared in her mind's eye, with SAD NEWS written in bright let-ters. Underneath it was a water crystal photo.

On February 5, 2018, Isabel called again and said she had been thinking about me so intensely over the past few days that she assumed I had followed Peter since she had not heard from me for weeks. I said, maybe you have been thinking about me because I am working on the water crystal book and keep wondering why they from the other side want the book to be called sad news and what tests I still have to do. Isa said to take half the picture where you are with Peter, wrap it around a bottle of distilled water and send it to Switzer-land. Peter wants you to grab a pen and paper and write everything down in shorthand. It's about the whole thing, nature, animals, people, everything. Above all, the earth is suffering from the Americanization of food. Although vegetarianism is trendy, global meat consumption is increasing dramatically, especially in the emerging economies of China and India. As a result, green-house gas emissions are rising, and H_2O is diminishing as more and more ani-mals require more and more. One kilogram of beef requires more than 15,000 liters! And increased animal excretions are producing more and more meth-ane. It is already responsible for one-fifth of greenhouse gas. That's more than the exhaust from all the planes, automobiles, and trains combined to produce.

And with the increasing factory farming and industrialization of agriculture, a few international companies will dominate the market." I said, "Well, that could be very problematic. It would lead to wars over water." "Yes, water scarcity and radioactive polluted water and soil from reactor accidents are the problems."

"Oh," I said, remembering that I had already interpreted my friend Renate's prophetic water crystal photo as a nuclear mushroom cloud. Dr. Renate Kaiser-Alexnat worked in Japan for a year as an agricultural scientist and is still in scientific contact with the land of smiles. She also wrote about it in "How Water Connects Our Worlds". When the Fukushima incident happened, I didn't even think about the water crystal photo and my interpretation. Only when I read Renate's report did I realize that the water crystal photo also was a prediction of water painters."

High-voltage disaster and dog connection - 1st test

As with an earlier experiment with Ernst Braun after my father's death, the next soul star experiment with my late husband was also a prophecy.

The WCP generated with a photo of my husband on the next page, which Mr. Braun was kind enough to give me, shows the dog (below with the black boomerang under his "arm") who had been on the iron chain for years. The owner released him at the end of February 2017 due to her illness. Tobi had lost his job as a guard dog and came to me to offer his services.

After all, I had offered it to him. Whenever I came by and spoiled him with treats, I would say, "If Lisbela is ever gone, you come to me."

So did he have no acclimatization problems at all? Everyone marveled at the perfect dog despite years of torture: Tobi had been on an iron chain around the clock for years.

The water crystal photo below shows a light bulb in the upper left corner above the triangle. It was a prophecy of the high-voltage disaster that destroyed several electrical devices and some light bulbs two months after the experiment, on April 24, 2017.

If we are allowed to dream prophetically or, as with the WKP, to look into the future, we may assume that our loved ones in the beyond still communicate with us and point out certain things to us.

Peter's four soul stars of the second experiment

On February 22, 2018, I felt nervous already in the morning. The dogs were happy because I suddenly took the long way to Fernanda. I cried again for a long time in her arms. I sobbed even more at the repeated força of my hearty egg lady, with which she comforted me. I never thought that after a year, it could be so bad again. When my parents moved to the astral plane, I did not suffer as much. Fernanda had already wondered why I hadn't been there for so long. After paying for the chicken and duck eggs, she cut me some kale fresh from the field and a large piece of a pumpkin. Her fowls roam freely and only spend the night behind bars. Later I biked to Tavira. There was a notification in the mailbox. The package turned out to be the 728-page book: "Die 64 Genschlüssel". The next visit was to the electricity company (EDP) to get reimbursed for my electronic equipment. EDP workers accidentally destroyed my electric appliances by serving high-voltage. After more than a year, EDP replaced part of my damages.

In the Evening, at choir rehearsal, I was tearful during the sad songs. Gabi, the teacher from Bremen, said that the grieving process should take six years. But I think there is no time limit. How long the grieving process and the individual stages take varies from person to person. When I checked my e-mails at home, Peter's soul stars beamed at me. At least they compensated me for this grave day.

The first beautifully shining crystal is a ring, a symbol of eternity, hope, and steadfastness. It is also a symbol of our infinite love. Is it a coincidence that Ernst Braun colored the enclosed ring yellow? Pure yellow is the color with the highest radiance s well as the strongest signal and long-range effect because we associate it with direct, shimmering sunlight. Of the warm colors, it is the least tangible and unreal. In Asia, therefore, it has always stood for the beautiful, the sacred, and the divine. Yellow means glow, radiance, the sun, and light. Yellow represents cheerfulness and optimism and a sharp mind and intellect. Other meanings of yellow are absolute truth, rationality, knowledge, and wisdom: "Clear head," "the light comes to me," and "enlightenment."

https://alpina-farben.de/artikel/farbsymbolik-bedeutung-gelb

Does it have to do with our encounter? On the night of February 17, 2017, a cheerfully radiant Peter had shown me his light-filled new surroundings, which reminded me of the yellow dune landscape of Erg Chebbi in Morocco. And that's where we wanted to be at that moment. While the camper was still long packed, the Piaggo was still in the back of the garage for years to come. Peter loved the desert almost as much as the sea.

The crystal also shows hexagons and crescents. The hexagon represents the harmonious development of physical, social and spiritual elements in human life and their integration into a perfect whole. It symbolizes the union of male and female, matter and spirit, to form a perfect whole.

The crescent moon symbolizes the feminine, mysterious power that is intuitive and not rational. I point to these themes in many books. When Peter was alive with me, he didn't read any of them. But now he seems to be aware of all of them. It became clear to me, among other things, when he allowed himself a joke on April 9, 1917 to cheer me up and show that he now also shares my metaphysical insights: When translating the book "Cranberry Power Fruit" (see p. 116) into German, I entered the last sentence for my readers in Google Translator: In the end, all that remains is to wish you all the best on your path to the light, to inner freedom, to serenity, and radiant health! Thank you for your trust! In place of the German translation, this text appeared:

In the end, the only thing will be, you're right, you're right, you're right, you're right. Thank you for your trust!

"Yes, Peter, I hope my confidence will help me get back on track. You have always doubted life after physical death. I told you, you would experience it, and you can trust it. I am glad that you now confirm it in such a multifaceted way.

When I re-entered it with a new window, it came right: "Am Ende ist alles, was noch zu wünschen übrig ist, Ihnen alles Gute auf Ihrem Weg ins Licht, zu innerer Freiheit, zu Gelassenheit und strahlender Gesundheit zu wünschen! Danke für Ihr Vertrauen!" (Meyer 2017)

At this point, I would like to answer all those readers who ask me why I no longer publish my books with a big publishing house but self-publish with BoD. It also has to do with a lack of trust. I discovered that my former publisher sold 2,000 copies of a book to a company without paying my honorarium or only two years later, after my request.

The upper right corner of Peter's second soul star seems to represent a childhood wish of mine. I always wanted a colored sister. I then had a brown inflatable Blinky-Winky doll with wiggly eyes. I put it in front of the window along with a lump of sugar cubes for the stork. Needless to say that my mother was not willing to take the necessary initiative.

I often told Peter about it, saying jokingly that I at least have a tan husband with a negro nose.

With the letters starting at the top left, I first thought of EBAY and a miscarriage of justice that I have reported in my biographical novels.

This theory is also supported by what Isabel Bannier-Groß told me through the media about Peter's friend Bolko Seifert, who was my lawyer in the case at the time and had died five years before Peter. But in the meantime, the Facebook scandal had come to light. And the letters are FB AX. Ax is English for an axe, but also something to chop, in the sense of shorten, abolish. I own a few shares, therefore the message. Probably Peter was only trying to give my book more substance with this prediction. Thank you, my dear!

Peter did not believe in his lifetime what he was experiencing now. Sooner or later, we will recognize the reality beyond our present consciousness. After all, we have not known for a long time that the structural elements of the atoms are not matter. It has already changed our perception and awareness of nature. And I hope that water crystal photography will also contribute to the expansion of consciousness.

The third shining soul star is similar to Cat Max's, where wisdom and inner clear-sightedness came to my mind. What I have already been able to experience with my husband since his death is truly a testimony to enlightenment. Writing "Beyond Death" was not only a need for me but a testimony of love: the reflections between people and moments, the fluid refractions and intrusions between fantasy and reality that we like to call coincidence for lack of explanation.

Looking at the water crystal on the following page at the lower left, I laughed out loud when I realized it represented my mother's second cousin. Peter was not pleased with all my enthusiasm in June 2009 when we discovered a kinship with the singing actress.

A fortune teller had told me in the early 1990s that I was related to Doris Day, but I didn't believe it at the time. Family tree surfing on the Internet was also not widespread at that time.

Doris was not Peter's cup of tea. That is made clear by the repulsive nature of her image on the WCP on the next page to the left of the light-covered figure in the dark corridor: chubby with cheeks, hydrogen blonde, and singing full-bodied. I imagine he had asked his Uncle Adolph to paint it in water: https://de.wikipedia.org/wiki/Adolph_Meyer_(Maler)

Peter was quite annoyed when I wrote a family novel for Doris about two world wars. I wanted her to get to know her Neckar relatives and how their lives might have turned out if her favorite grandmother had not emigrated to the US. The writing hadn't bothered Peter much. But whenever I googled something, I shared it with him.

At the time, Doris was still the most successful box-office diva of all time behind some male colleagues. But she didn't get an Oscar, not even for her life's work: 39 movies! In "Family Code", you can read why. I also showed him new pictures in which Doris looked like my mother. To illustrate this, I quote the passage from "Family Code" in which my aunt called me to tell me the news:*".... And how are we supposed to be related to Doris Day? Anneliese replied: Hilde Wiswesser said, through our grandmother. What was her name? Eleonore Nollert. How does Hilde know that? She says it's official. You can check with the Mückenloch municipality ... ".*

"I was delighted, moved, honored, a vibrant mix of feelings. About a woman whose song Que sera almost everyone in the world knows. I filled the google search bar with the name of the singer and actress. Did you hear my conversation with Anneliese? You must be talking to a relative of... wow... still the most successful actress of all time! On Quigley's "All Time Number One Stars" list, Tom Cruise is No. 1, and Doris Day is No. 6, right behind her friend, the Carmel mayor.

Peter grumbled, not rambling on. To his mocking grin, I said, how would you act if you were related to John Wayne?

Your relationship with that woman won't earn us a penny.

Money, money, I groaned.

Yes, Peter replied gruffly, we'd better concentrate on business.

Ah! The family tree. That is indeed her grandmother Anna Christina, or her great-grandmother?

A Nollert like my great-grandmother. They are nine years apart, probably sisters. Endorphins shot through my veins.

Peter worried: So what?

I get excited: My mother is probably her second cousin.

So, does that get us anywhere?

I: Neckarhäuserhof doesn't have much more than a dozen houses.

Peter worried: Don't you have anything better to do?

I: Ma is only two months younger than Doris. Of all the distant cousins, she is the most like her, at least in looks and singing. Anneliese and Hilde are more like comedians.

Peter: You make me sick. If you don't stop, I'm going to leave. We've got the stress with the Ubbe asshole, and you're wasting your time with this kind of bullshit. Hey, wait a minute, I shot back: You are the one who always gives the money to the scammers." (Meyer 2016, p. 43).

Peter's aversion explains the unsympathetic picture of Doris when she usually let portrays herself in a very appealing way.

Revealing is also that the WCP does not show her chocolate side. Doris almost always had herself photographed in the right profile.

The soul star on the previous page still shows a laughing grimace above the head of the former movie star.

That is probably supposed to be Peter laughing at his joke. As he always did when he adorned himself with an original headdress to make me laugh: Mom's crocheted doilies, boxes, pillows, pot holders etc.

How do the water artists see the new home in France?

Maurits, the new man in my life, has bought a one-hundred-year-old house in France. That was again an opportunity for me to ask the spiritual world to give their input into the water. The poster of the most meaningful crystal was also a good opportunity for an original birthday gift for Maurits' 70th, which was also the anniversary of the death of his wife Lucie.

E. Braun wrapped the following photo around a vial filled with water. The test ran under "Soul stars of the house inhabitants". By the way, I had Googled the deceased owner. He died at the age of 88 on May 5, the day Maurits and I had gotten to know each other better. Maurits' mother gave birth to ten children, so there used to live almost as many people in the Hagenaar house as in the Tixier house. Since some of the water crystal photos show ghostly beings, some relatives may still be present. Perhaps they need the help of sensitives to facilitate their transition to the spiritual world.

After all, they cannot evolve if they remain attached to the earthly plane. However, it may be that some WCPs represent the former inhabitants because the title was not "Soul stars of the house inhabitants".

Peter and Lucie check in with us from time to time; the last time when we visited the dentist Wolfgang Spengler in São Brás, who is also a sculptor. Maurits and Lucie had already been interested in the Great Soul, made of orange wood with round glasses. But it was too expensive for him (or for her?). Now Maurits decided to buy the Gandhi statue. As we were saying goodbye, the alarm of my smartphone's watch, which was in the handbag at the entrance, suddenly turned on. But I had never used that function before!

Years ago, I heard from the painting medium Gasparetto or Henri de Toulouse-Lautrec, respectively, who was channeled through him, that the spiritual world can communicate with us through electrical devices. Many people do not even notice their loved ones' contact, for example, via light signs, radio or TV messages, as I have experienced with my grandmother, father, mother, husband and more.

You could already see on page 39 in a video how Antonio Gasparetto channels in trance Old Masters. The following video shows how Antonio Gasparetto also speaks French in the trance state. Or in other words, you can see and hear the Old Master painting using Gasparetto's hands and vocal cords.

https://www.youtube.com/watch?v=bWpc71VKiDI

But back to the house, to France and our beyond spouses. Perhaps the two of them even chose it. Because, Peter and Lucie both loved France. Two years ago, Maurits' daughter and her husband bought a house near the one we're looking at here. Whenever we drove through the country, Peter delighted in the magnificent avenues and pretty villages.

In the following water crystal, less accomplished painters were at work than, for example, on page 51, where Peter looks as in a photograph. Two cubic heads of different sizes are looking at each other in profile. A dog sits in front of the left large head, probably to indicate that Maurits is now Tobi's official owner. He has insured him, after all.

On the next WCP, you can see the roof where it had burned on the left side. It is the thickest part. Replacing the roof could cost up to 30,000 EUR. Hopefully, the three chunks do not mean other projects on the house, heating, water piping, mold, etc. Many TV shows give sufficient insights into the expensive surprises which house buyers can count.

On the brilliant crystal on page 93, many people appear ghostly in the center. Some of the ex-residents would possibly recognize themselves. But if they should be ghosts, then hopefully only good ones. All crystals radiate light and cheerfulness, though a few insides appear nebulous. A face I can also imagine in the upper prong. Maybe Lucie, the radiant one?

In the center, I think I recognize a chain of links, but it could also be people chained together. A chain connects something and often represents a connection between two opposite poles. *The chain is, therefore, frequently a symbol of the relations between heaven and earth.*

https://symbolonline.de/index.php?title=Kette

You can find my connection to the beyond in all my books. That there are more things between heaven and earth than the school wisdom teaches, I have suffi-ciently explained in it. On the upper left prong I see a "6" and a "0". Saint-Ger-vais-d'Auvergne's zip code begins with a six and ends with a zero, the same as Michelstadt. The top right prong shows a heart, and above I see a cat, symbolizing my love for cats. In the lower right prong, I can make out a head. I don't see much else at the moment. But as already said, we recognize many messages only later, especially if they are prophetic.

The Beekeeper in France

Maurits and I both have green thumbs, but the love of nature is even more distinct in the ¾ Dutch and ¼ German. In his homeland, Maurits is called the bee man. He had almost seventy bee boxes and sold the honey from his bees in the neighborhood.

In Portugal, he had less luck with honey-producing builders. The following water crystal photo shows an eye-pleasing hexagon, nature's favorite figure.

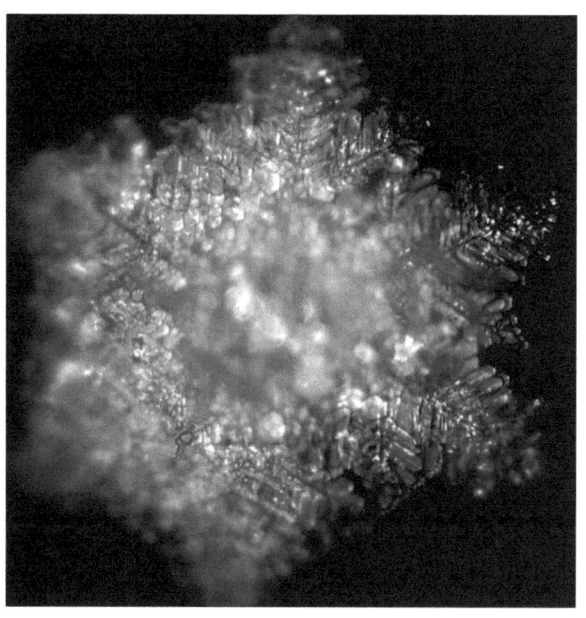

The hexagon demonstrates the bee's work as it closes the house into the perfect hexagon with the last, sixth wall.

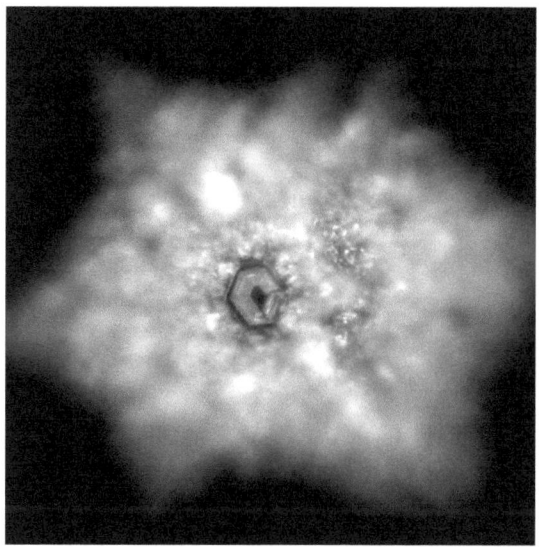

Perhaps this crystal image means that the bees in France will be busy building again. Maurits, after all, wants to take his bee boxes to the Grande Nation. I'm glad that in the spring of 2021, we'll find the house in good, easy-to-renovate condition and won't be bothered at all by any ghosts that may be present. Our two blessed spouses and all our loved ones will independently accompany us and protect us from possible spiritual assaults.

VII. THE HIDDEN LIGHT IN OUR DNA

A few years ago, I had the privilege of proofreading Richard Rudd's book, The Golden Path, for Jim Humble Publishing. That sparked my interest in another of the author's works: "Die 64 Genschlüssel: Das Öffnen der verborgenen höheren Bestimmung in unserer DNA." (Gene Keys: Unlocking the Higher Purpose Hidden in Your DNA)

Repressed memories

The Gene Keys is a system that links our DNA to the symbolism of the ancient Chinese divination system, I Ching. It contains 64 key identification codes representing specific processes in human spiritual development based on the language of archetypes or a kind of genetic memory we carry in our blood. So we harbor in our bodies the whole evolutionary memory of humanity. C.G. Jung called it the collective unconscious. Rudd speaks of the repository of human karma or evolutionary artifacts. But these are not (yet) or only readable by a few. They are repressed memories that correspond to unencoded DNA, also called junk DNA. They are said to make up 98% of our genome! (Rudd 2016, p. 491)

I think I was guided to this book. It has to do with the fact that my hologenetic profile has exactly the gene key that made me deal with my shadowy action products some 35 years ago. During the California health boom of the 1980s, I had prophetic and past life dreams due to a cleansing process. We had a German 2nd manager in our apartment complex in Hermosa Beach who approached me about my prophetic dream.

I had dreamed that Peter's mother had died. I once quoted the conversation from my autobiographical novel Family Code: "Have you ever had a dream in which you were another person? No, Walter replied, not that I know of. 'What about you? 'Yes, recently. I have experienced more metaphysical things in this apartment than I have in the last ten years. I must have been a shepherd boy in my previous life. Why do you think that? In the past two weeks, I first had the dream where I was a shepherd boy being killed, then I was a woman with a

Quaker hat like the one on the 2-cent stamp and my husband was killed in the Civil War, then a murderous gladiator, a Jewish girl in the ghetto, an English-speaking actor living in a hotel, a very beautiful blonde woman being pushed on a ladder wagon and having a hard life, a fat Polynesian being feathered and tarred. Walter: Wow. Not very nice lives. I think in my last life I was the shepherd. Why? Because my last dream was the same as the first when I was shot in the back. Whoa, not very good lives. You should have a better one this time (Meyer 2016, p. 97). Yes, indeed, I have had many positive experiences in this life of mine so far.

What can the gene keys do for us?

The gene keys in my hologenetic profile could help me see some light about myself. But it was a dream that inspired me to write this chapter: My mother called and told me to come to her. It seemed urgent. Although I planned to fly to the U.S., I went to my mother first and met her along with three other women. She said she didn't have time now and that I should wait. After I woke up, I thought about the meaning of this dream. Since nighttime visions can symbolize, among other things, the dreamer's unconscious shadow sides, something came to mind. I had often invited my cousin Heide who has my mother's features, to visit me. Because of her fear of flying, I had said she could fly back with me when I went to Germany in the summer. But I had forgotten about it again, especially since she hadn't said anything. Heide never spoke to me again, even when we met her at a side meeting at a café in Eberbach and drove her home. She showed us her huge vegetable garden. Even if I had thought of my offer, it would not have occurred to me to ask her in this dry summer. But she reminded me later, piqued.

After all, the 64 gene keys mostly have to do with our shadow sides. Therefore, since the dream also had to do with flying, I think it was to draw attention to my shadow or my challenge of superficiality in evolution (see diagram). I need to shut up more. I probably could never have placed the dream had I not delved into the 64 gene keys. So now, through contemplation, hopefully, I can gradually turn my shadows into light. I don't know if my life will be enough for that. But it is something to acknowledge and accept the dark sides.

The 64 gene keys are about finding the genetically predetermined life path according to the hologenetic profile created by specifying place and time of birth. Here you can have your profile created for free:

https://teachings.genekeys.com/free-profile

You can see what something like this might look like in the table on the next page. By the way: You do not have to give your name when you request your hologenetic profile. When you spiritually engage with your gene keys, universal consciousness traits, shadow frequencies and gifts according to your profile, you can tap into your inner being and activate your higher destiny. It's not easy, and it doesn't happen quickly. Also, the 728-page book is not proofread or is poorly proofread. Nevertheless, it is delightful to dig in.

Perhaps my friend Barbara Simonsohn, who also introduced me to Windpferd Publishing, only made contact so that I would delve into my gene keys. Because after proofreading "Goldener Pfad," I asked for a break. And after buying "Die 64 Genschlüssel" and sinking into it, I didn't get another editing job. I will also be careful not to ask for work. Precisely because I have the experience

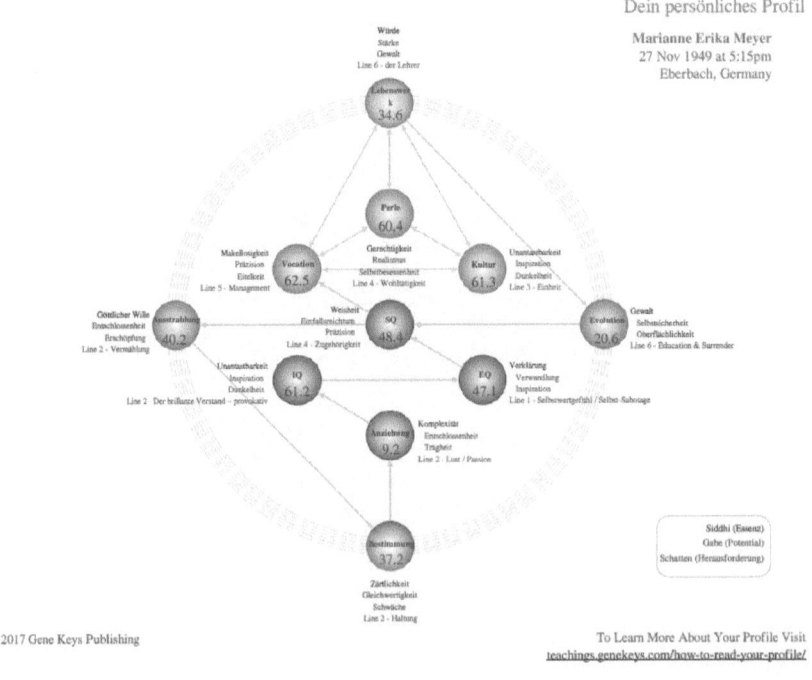

that everything I need comes to me automatically. That started with my birth with pliers. Since then, I have let everything happen to me. I am someone who lives in the day and waits for what comes. My whole path in life is pavred with these so-called coincidences. My ex-boyfriend, who was still trying, persuaded me to go out with him. That's how I met my baron, whom I introduced to art. I think that was my doing because shortly after that, our relationship ended. An innkeeper called me and said, I have a guest here looking for a model for clothes and shoes for his newspaper. That's how I met my fiancé, who took me to Frankfurt. That must have been his job. Because after that we were together for only a short time. By chance, I met my classmate who motivated me to study education. So I quit my job at Deutsche Bank AG.

The executive secretary wasn't my thing anyway. All that interested me was that it was the education department, that the library adjoined my office and that the view from the 18th floor of the Selmi skyscraper over Frankfurt was magnificent. The following coincidence was that I met my ex-fiancé's friend at my first demo. This Wilhelmshaven-born Heinz-Peter sent me to the other Wilhelmshaven-born Claus-Peter, with whom I lived together for almost 44 years until he transitioned to the spiritual world. The so-called coincidences multiplied. Because Heinz Peter Gerhardt, retired professor of Freire peda-gogy, who is still alive, lives in the Algarve! He had recently told me that I should travel and lecture like him. I said I would fall off the meat. I would nev-er get off the toilet because of stage fright. He just said, "Oh, we all have that problem. This conversation has been going through my head for a while. But maybe I'm jumping over my shadow because I assume it was HP's job to give me a push this time, too. My behavior of being led is also genetic, and I found it on page 228 in the 20th gift of self-confidence.

We all could follow our intended path through contemplation on the gene keys how much our trained way of thinking influences us. Then no more fear must affect our mental strength.

In my book "Survival Aid for All Viral infections" you will find out more about how to cope with your fears. Another content is the principle of shaping your reality by recognizing what you want. It shows that doing what you love makes yourself and others happy. That is what makes all of us happy and con-tent. And that is our challenge.

VIII. EXPERIENCES AFTER DEATH

Communication with the deceased

Of the many studies on afterlife experiences, the one by Judy and Bill Guggenheim stands out. In their book "Hello From Heaven!: A New Field of Research - After-Death Communication - Confirms That Life and Love Are Eternal", more than two thousand vividly describe their unforgettable communications with loved ones in the afterlife. About half of all widowed people experience this phenomenon, and there is an immediate sense of presentness of the deceased. I had it with my husband right after I left the hospital morgue. Despite being in shock, I had a thought transmission that all was well and that Peter would help me better now than in the flesh. I also had a spontaneous after-death experience after my father discarded his body. We had friends over to play cards. My producer loved to play cards. As we sat at the table, a blissful connection feeling overcame me. I felt a deep love and warmth.

But my most satisfying experiences after death were with my husband on the 6th and 11th day posthum. First, Peter took me by the hand and showed me his new surroundings. It looked like Morocco, where we were supposed to be going. But he was wearing the T-shirt and Bermudas he wore in California when he almost got shot. The book "The 64 Ways: Personal Contemplations on the Gene Keys", says that the 60th siddhi enables a person to travel through time and space. So far, it has only happened to me spontaneously that I left my body. But I have met people who consciously abandoned their bodies after meditation to visit family members or friends. Afterwards, they told them on the phone what they had observed. (Family Code p. 142)

The second time, Peter came into my bedroom. I awoke to a knock and was about to reach for the knife on the nightstand - probably genetically conditioned by a previous life as a Legionnaire - when I saw Peter standing at the end of the bed. He was wearing the gray sweater I had knitted myself. Peter looked even more youthful than the first time. He beamed, and I flew into his arms. After he left, I could still feel the velvet wool on my hands. And every time after such an experience, I feel serene and filled with inner peace and joy for days.

On June 6, 2011, it would have been my mother's 87th birthday, I woke up and heard my mother, who had died on January 1, 2011, say in her bell-bright soprano: Dass mer des net vergesse. I felt her over my shoulder against my cheek. The day before, I had told my sister-in-law that I would visit Ännchen on my way back from the dentist. I went to my mother's friend; she was pleased when I told her about this experience.

In the chapter on sympathy for deceased loved ones, I have already told about the after-death contact with my grandmother, whom I'd suddenly noticed by her smell while sitting at the PC. My cousin Karin even saw her husband leaning against a tree at his funeral. He continued to haunt her house like a poltergeist for a year. Even when Karin had guests, the key would suddenly rattle, you would hear footsteps on the stairs, and the smell of his eau de toilette hung in the air. My mother saw my father when she was in the bathtub. He was naked and all white. He also showed his white sole. This color represents innocence, purity, and perfection. I interpreted this to mean that all my father's actions in earthly life were right, according to the standards of the Beyond, even, as I later learned from my brother, that he did not comply with earthly laws.

I had most of my personal spiritual experiences on my PC because that is where I spend most of my time and write leisurely. I especially had a lot of contact with my husband, as you can read in "Über den Tod." I also had post-death contact with my mother-in-law without having known her obituary. I reported on this in "Family Code" on p. 101ff.

I had another special moment of happiness. In the morning I put water in the kettle. Since I wanted it to boil for 5 minutes, I set it to the lowest temperature. I forgot that the kettle was still steaming, I tried to fill my cup with water, but it came in a gush over my left hand. I expected severe pain but was surprised it even didn't feel hot. My hand had not burned at all! It was similar to the fire walk in Venice, California, when we set fire to a high pyre and then walked over the glowing coals. Then I also felt like I was walking over charcoal, fresh out of the bag. The temperature was neutral! My hand didn't turn red either, and I didn't feel the slightest pain. I am always amazed at the ability of the spiritual world to help us, and I am always grateful for the services of the guardian angel. I think it was my husband because he knew I had already suffered a lot in the household. I burned myself like that more than once. Because of my recklessness, Peter never let me handle the tree saw. Every time I asked him to teach me something, he reminded me of the bread machine to which I had once lost the tip of my finger. Anyway, this morning's moment of happiness made my day more beautiful. On June 23, I unrolled 4-5 pieces of paper from the toilet paper roll and discovered a fresh blood heart on the penultimate piece. Although I had to stretch my arms upward so my head was down and it couldn't be my blood, I immediately unrolled some more paper and carefully tried to blow my nose, but there was no blood. I immediately thought of the oregano plant Renate had given me the day before. There was a little card inside that drew attention to the Sáo Pedro. But on the Internet, I learned that St. Peter's is on June 29. Then I remembered that it was the birthday of Peter's daughter-in-law, his friend's youngest daughter, who crashed fifty years and nine days ago. I congratulated her and told her about the experience. When I heard or read about weeping statues and bleeding Madonnas, I always thought, well, who knows what the believers saw there? After this experience, I am no longer so sceptical. By the way, I immediately took a picture of the heart-shaped spot when it was still bright red and emailed the pic to the birthday girl.

It would be interesting to photograph such Madonna tears microscopically or examine the DNA. In any case, I welcome such messages from the higher realms of consciousness. It makes me happy not to be alone, despite my loneliness. But only through the information from my gene keys did I realize why I remember past lives and am in touch with the spiritual world. It's in my genes! See chapter: What can the gene keys do for us? It's also that I act as a kind of educational representative. With each new book, I want to help my readers to recognize their full potential. We are all born with talents and tasks, and it is the greatest happiness when we acknowledge our destiny.

If we were all guided and gratefully accepting everything and acting according to our gifts, we could live much happier and more peaceful lives.

After-effects of post-mortem contacts

At the moment of death, the soul can contact loved ones, even if they are far away. Often, these do not even know that their relatives are dead. But Berlin death researcher Bernard Jakoby says, "There are numerous reports of experiencing the presence or appearance of a deceased person at the moment of death."

Usually, the dying are prepared and accompanied days or weeks beforehand, usually by deceased friends or relatives. But few share this with their families. My father knew this, too, or he would not have labeled his 1998 folder by the end of September 98. He passed away on October 1. Bolko Seifert, born five minutes before Peter in the same delivery room, collapsed while walking, just like Peter. He had also prepared his friend. A few days before Peter passed away, I sat with Peter in front of the TV after midnight, although I usually go to bed at 10 p.m. Suddenly he said, "Look! There are grains with gray letters on the television. Intuitively, I said, that looks like a ghost message. Maybe Bolko is trying to tell us something. The ghostly silence that followed should have warned me, but that's probably when my defense mechanism of repression kicked in. On other occasions, Peter would have made disparaging remarks about my paranormal experiences. This time he said nothing and kept zapping. But seeing Peter lying so peacefully in the hospital morgue gave me the intense feeling that all was well - clearly a thought transference.

The deceased, freed from earthly burdens, have a relaxed facial expression immediately after death, but they often worry about their loved ones. Therefore, they appear in dreams or contact their relatives by radio, telephone, and PC, but also show themselves in rare cases. They want their loved ones to see that they are still around, although in another dimension. Many who have crossed over want to help their relatives sort things out or reconcile with them. Sometimes I feel watched when I stand up. That is a clear sign that Peter is showing me that he is still there and I should feel loved and safe. I often sense love, inner peace and an indescribable lightness. Also, during events and celebrations, many of our loved ones are present in the afterlife. They want to participate and rejoice with us. They connect to us through the bond of love.

In the case of my older friend Hilde, whose husband came to the USA with Wernher von Braun as a rocket aircraft developer and whom she cared for eight years with Alzheimer's, it was like this: Heinz often came to her bedside and talked to her. But only as long as Hilde was single. When she married the actor John Hudson at age 69, Heinz never let her see him again. (Meyer 2016). The deceased want to provide comfort. But many after-death contacts happen years or decades after death when the bereaved are no longer grieving. Peter contacted me just six days after his passing.

As a result of after-death contacts, loved ones may find hidden treasures or important papers they didn't know. Using tarot cards in conjunction with an AM/FM frequency scanning radio (PSB7 ITC Research Device) given to me by a friend, ghosts directed me to search a shed for a file Peter's brother later found. Also, messages in post-mortem contacts can sometimes protect or warn the person of suicide or undetected illnesses, accidents, or crimes.

I think it's good that today in Europe, we can talk more openly than we used to about these contacts with deceased loved ones without being looked at with suspicion. In the 1980s, it was different. We were already living in California, where almost everyone knew about true dreams and past lives because family members or friends already had after-death contacts. Whenever I flew to Germany and talked about a past life, I looked into rolling eyes or smug smiling faces. Yet it would be great for everyone to work on the shadows of the past. It would reduce prejudices. In regressions of past lives, we usually remember less pleasant lives. Joyful, conflict-free, comfortable, and happy situations don't have to be processed or worked.

The water crystal pictures are also clear after-death contacts for me. What else would they be? Just think of the predictions of Peter's water crystal pictures: Dog, light bulb, Facebook, or the WCP with the caricature of Doris Day!

For me there is no doubt that water is a medium to connect the spiritual and physical worlds. Water does not imprint itself. We in this world affect the water with our feelings, our vibrations. This was made clear above all by Masaru Emoto and his team. But only through the tests with Ernst Braun did it become clear to me that water is also quasi the canvas on which the spiritual painters can show us that their art is not lost. They can still work, although on other levels with higher frequencies. In this respect, shouldn't the study of water crystal photography be a scientific endeavor? After all, it is nothing other than what parapsychology deals with, i.e. science cannot explain occult phenomena in the first place. My explanation for the water crystal images is that they are messages from our deceased. See also experiences after death from page 98! The videos of Gasparetto also show how the old masters painted through him: https://www.youtube.com/watch?v=URM8KGpjztE.

Closing Remarks and Acknowledgements

Our loved ones in the afterlife want to tell us that they are still active on another plane of being. They want to help or warn us or only be there for us. And to return to the comment so often heard about laying the dead to rest: The dead are the ones who contact us, often before the bereaved have even learned of their loved one's death. That has been proven thousands of times in countless studies on communication after death.

 That we continue to exist on a higher frequency level after we leave our physical shell behind is undeniable to me. I am in active contact with this other world. Why this is so, I have discovered in the book "The 64 Gene Keys". That the souls of the artists communicate with us through the water is also beyond question for me. Whether you see it the same way after reading and especially after looking at the water crystal photos, I don't know. But I hope the WCPs interpretation didn't confuse you too much. I wonder what our loved ones in the afterlife aim at with their communication efforts. Has it always been like this, or does it have to do with the critical time of humanity? Perhaps these extraordinary discoveries, such as water crystal photography and gene keys, are a wake-up call. I imagine the crystal images are to make us aware that there is something beyond materialism, greed, addictions, and hatred. Our society must free itself from this.

 The WCP also show our dark sides. I believe that if we accept and transform our dark sides, we can bring about a change toward more tolerance and charity through deep inner understanding. That is already happening, for example, when schools invite Holocaust survivors to speak about the horrors of Nazi terror. It would also be good if American citizens were more aware of films like Sonia Kennebeck's documentary "National Bird." In it, three war veterans tell their stories about the U.S. Air Force's drone program. Their complicity in killing unknown and seemingly innocent people in faraway war zones gives the whistleblowers no peace.

It would also be healing for veterans to tell schools why they return from war zones as broken men and women. That could be very healing for them and help the peace process. If U.S. citizens knew the orders their husbands, fathers, brothers, and friends received and the atrocities they committed that plunged them into the most severe emotional conflict, their loved ones might be more likely to help them cope with guilt and shame. I first became aware of this when I talked with my friend from northern Germany about how much the soldiers who fought in Vietnam must have suffered. Sigrid told me about a severely depressed acquaintance who confided to his brother how they lured the children into the village with chocolate and then shot them. Speaking of which, Sigrid, as a seven-year-old, was an eyewitness to the consequences of the Allied war crimes against the civilian population of Hamburg. As a seven-year-old, she had seen some of the 40,000 corpses shriveled by phosphorus bombs.

We should better accept our shadows, wake up and realize who we are, where we come from and where we are going. Then we will also recognize how important it is to take the necessary conservation of resources seriously. The earth is not a self-service store. Climate protection must be on the political agenda, and EVERYONE must be able to share in the benefits of globalization. It is about balancing social imbalances. Just as an over-acidified environment in the body is the ideal breeding ground for germs and cancer to thrive, so does an imbalance in the world cause conflict. Social injustice, lying politicians and compliant media always lead to imbalance, often unrest, corruption and war. Germans are also blinded. Very few know that Germany is now the state with the lowest private family wealth and the third lowest pension entitlements of all euro countries. That's why it's my concern to inform my readers about things they don't learn through the mainstream media or their elected representatives.

In Portugal, for example, where incomes are far below those in Germany, people are much more likely to live in their own homes. While I have never received notice to vacate an apartment, I imagine it would be terrible.

If Europe is to function, social security must be equal. It cannot be that some euro states grant their pensioners a basic pension while the pensioners of the main net contributor go home empty-handed. The latter often spend their twilight years abroad because they cannot live freely and independently on their small pensions in Germany.

In addition to the unification of social systems, it will also be necessary for the future to unite art and metaphysics with science. It is essential to recognize that all living beings, whether snowdrops, heather snails or Homo sapiens, are animated by light energy. How we humans deal with this power is crucial. Seekers are in a quandary because the church conceals some things and scientists avoid proving the soul. Among the laudable exceptions are such figures as the respected psychiatrists Elisabeth Kübler-Ross and Raymond A. Moody, as well as those mentioned above. But by and large, science has failed to extend its field of inquiry into the spiritual realm. We should believe that at the root of being is no such thing as being at all, even though we constantly encounter the soul. We feel love, the driving force of being.

I would be happy if the water crystal photography inspired you. If you would like to experiment with soul stars or soul shaping yourself, I would be grateful for your experiences via email: drmarianneemeyer @ gmail.com

Thank you so much for your trust! Now I wish that more people may consider it their task to make our highly technical and networked world of upheaval more human. I would be happy if I succeeded in conveying to you that we need not fear death. With water painting, electricity, reiki, automatic writing, telepathy, etc., we can still draw attention to ourselves and contribute even after we leave our bodies: without the strains of a suffering body.

First and foremost, I thank my beloved husband, Claus-Peter Meyer, who passed from this life to another on Feb 11, 2017. Furthermore, I thank Bolko Seifert, born only 20 minutes earlier in the same delivery room as Peter but had already collapsed while walking in July 2012, just like my husband. Bolko, who proofread one of my Spirulina books during his lifetime, had medially shown Isabel Bannier-Groß the book SAD NEWS on Feb 28, 2017 and inspired me to write the same. My thanks to Isabel, who, thanks to her mediumistic powers, let me communicate with Peter on the 11th posthumous day and supported me spiritually and morally. I also thank Isabel's blessed father, Peter

Gross, who followed my husband into the afterlife on Sep 11, 2017. He had emailed me at the right moment the water crystal photos of his tap water before and after activation, which led me to Ernst F. Braun. Thanks also to the intuitive Swiss and his equally gifted daughter Sarah Steinmann, who brought me the soul stars from the sky. Through the work of the two water artists, I metaphorically conveyed what I have long known from experience: the spiritual world is constantly striving to support us and communicate with us. THANK YOU!

The spiritual world has perhaps chosen me for this intangible field of knowledge because of my metaphysical experiences. On my mother's side second sight has appeared through all generations. Thus, they expected fewer doubts of me, which would block the research urge. I thank my relatives and friends in this world and beyond. I also thank Christine Kittler, Dr. Kaiser-Alexnat, Renate Janzen, Sigrid Brennecke, Rudi and Hedwig Müller, Daniel, Evelyn, and Elisabeth Fleischer. The latter showed me the result of a strange nocturnal death contact. During separation from her unfaithful husband, she had once felt cold, as if a ghost was in the house, and strange noises. The thick, heavy glass bowl, the gift of a friend with the same fate, broke on the sideboard without any intervention. My cousin, Heide Bayer, whom I also thank, asked: Who had lived in this house before, and how had this person died? Indeed, the previous owner, a leather manufacturer from Offenbach, had cheated on his wife, and she had poisoned herself from grief.

That is further proof that we continue to exist after leaving the body. On Feb 16, 2018, I learned by chance from the mechanic of the Tavira company Confort, who repaired my hot water boiler, still from a post mortem contact. I had shown him the cover of "Beyond Death" with Peter's photo with a Harley cap and said, "You may have known him. Peter was in your store a lot." He said, "Yes, I did. The cap always reminded me of my military days. I served in the Navy. Do you think then that your husband is still with you?" Yes, I said. I told him about the clear evidence: The clairvoyant Isabel Groß called me from near Hanover. During the conversation, she said, "Peter is there right now, showing me you in black leggings and a long-sleeved top, painting something. I see the colors blue and yellow. Three days before, I was wearing my painting clothes and embellishing the blue and yellow tiled cistern with a brush. No one could know about it. The technician, thanks to him, too, told me about his wife's friend whose husband had died. He had taken out insurance, but his wife didn't even know. Her blessed husband, however, was able to tell her post-humously where he had kept the insurance policy, which she then found.

My thanks also go to other acquaintances and friends who reported their visual and auditory experiences with their loved ones on the other side and other extrasensory perceptions. We could fill another book with their insights. They testify to the fact that we can all use our mediumistic abilities. I also thank Anneliese Umbreit for the psychic experience, I had during an overnight stay at her house. It was the night before the funeral of her life partner Erich. I had tried in vain for hours to fall asleep. Suddenly I heard the water rushing. I thought: Why is she taking a shower in the middle of the night? It wouldn't stop. Odd, since Anneliese is usually so frugal. When I confronted her in the morning, she said, "It wasn't me. That could only have been Erich. He always took so many showers.

I could tell more haunted stories I have experienced myself or in my mother's family. But most of them can be found in my autobiographical novel "Family Code". Perhaps you would like to share your experiences with me and see them published in the next book. A reader from Reutlingen has already written me a long letter about her experiences with her loved ones in the afterlife, especially with her childhood sweetheart. I was happy about it. Especially about this paragraph: "In 2014, I went to a renowned medium because I had concerns whether I bind him too much to me and he should be somewhere else. But he gave me the answer, I had nothing to worry about, everything was fine, and it was his free will. He had chosen this path so that we could be together forever." That's how I see it with Peter, too. I suggested Mrs. K also write a book. It's time to open up to something like contact with our loved ones on the other side. And nothing is more meaningful and conclusive than your own experiences. In this context, I thank all spiritual helpers for their water art and the corresponding and encouraging manipulations on the PC! Whether Adolf Meyer-Gauting, Jochen Gestering, the Dembinskis, or ET are the painters of the WCP, I do not know. Jochen could be because I talked with him about the metaphysical after the death of his Nora. And his son has dedicated his dissertation

"German Pessimism and Indian Philosophy: A Hermeneutic Reading" to this topic.

We best remain open and curious about everything. If we are willing to explore new things, we also offer the "dead" possibilities to contact us: via radio, TV, PC, telephone and medial people. Or we receive signals via sight, hearing, smell, and thinking (telepathy), via bones and tissues.

I wish you, dear readers, that you realize your dreams and that we all make our wishes come true. For it is now time to realize that which is alive within us. The strongest and noblest motive of scientific research, the most sublime feeling of which we are capable, is the experience of the mystical. To whom this feeling is foreign, who can no longer marvel and lose himself in awe, is already dead in the soul. The knowledge that the inexplicable exists and reveals itself as the highest truth and most radiant beauty, of which we can only have a faint inkling - this knowledge and intuition are the core of religiosiy.

This would not only be Einstein's kind of religiosity. Also, Leonardo da Vinci would probably have agreed with this and would have been pleased with Goethe's opening poem and Einstein's quotation.

Water crystals and da Vinci's prophecy

I am happy to mention at the end the great master of genuine science and arts. As early as the 15th century, he suspected a wondrous new world hidden in water, which we discover only in future centuries. To him, frozen panes resembled living leaves, flowers and grasses: as if nature had prophetic dreams of plant life in the world of ice crystals.

Five-hundred years ago, Leonardo da Vinci saw no way to explain such a phenomenon with reason. His assumption was that other energies unknown to man existed besides the attraction of grated amber and the magnet (Merejcovski 1938).

He was right!

For it is our inherent energy that connects us to all living things. When we become aware of this all-encompassing power of love, we have a real chance of transforming the impending apocalypse into something we humans have been striving for since time immemorial: heaven on earth, the lost paradise.

Literatur

Braun, Ernst F.: Wasserkristalle. Zauberwelt aus gefrorenen Wassertropfen. AT-Verlag 2004

Dutschk, Otto, Die Energie der Seele. Bergisch-Gladbach 1999

Emoto, Masaru: The Message of Water. Die Antwort des Wassers, Burgrain 2002

Einstein, Albert: Autobiographisches. P. A. Schilpp (Hrsg.), Chicago 1979

Faulstich, Joachim, Das heilende Bewusstsein. München 2006, S. 59 ff

Jürgenson, Friedrich: Sprechfunk mit Verstorbenen. Praktische Kontaktherstellung mit dem Jenseits. München, 7. Aufl. 9/92

Merejcovski, Mitri, The Romance of Leonardo Da Vinci, New York 1938

Meyer, Marianne E.: Wunderwesen Wasser. Norderstedt 2002
    Family-Code, Norderstedt 2017
    Beyond Death. Death Is Not The End. Norderstedt 2017

Netherton, Morris, Shiffrin, Nancy: Bericht vom Leben vor dem Leben. Schirner 2005

Rudd, Richard: Der goldene Pfad: Eine Reise zur Selbsterleuchtung durch die Genschlüssel. Jim-Humble-Verlag 2018
    Die 64 Genschlüssel: Das Öffnen der verborgenen höheren Bestimmung in unserer DNA. Jim-Humble-Verlag 2015

Rýzl, Milan: Der Tod ist nicht das Ende. Von der Unsterblichkeit geistiger Energie. Augsburg 2005

Sheldrake, Rupert: Das schöpferische Universum. Berlin 1993

Shioya, Bobuo. Der Jungbrunnen des Dr. Shioya, 2. Aufl., Burgrain

Ter Riet, G. et al. Is Placebo analgesia mediated by endogenous opiods? A systematic review, Pain 1998, S. 76

Wolff, Hans Günter: Unsere Hunde - gesund durch Homöopathie: Heilfibel eines Tierarztes Stuttgart 2012

zaronews.world/zaronews-presseberichte/verbotene-erfindungen-energie-aus-dem-nichts-geniale-erfinder-verspottet-behindert-und-ermordet/

Excursus: Free energy for free people

"Nature understands no jesting; she is always true, always serious, always severe; she is always right, and the errors and faults are always those of man. The man incapable of appreciating her, she despises; and only to the apt, the pure, and the true, does she resign herself and reveal her secrets."

Johann Wolfgang von Goethe

Deep down, we know we can't keep doing what we're doing. Every day, 150 species become extinct. Growth, come hell or high water, is destroying our planet. As I show in "How Water Connects Our Worlds", there have long been ingenious inventors who can and have used water to build cars and make free energy usable with their machines.

As early as 1875, the visionary author Jules Verne had his novel character Cyrus Smith express his joy about a coal-free future through the principle of electrolysis - the electrical splitting of water - in "The Mysterious Island": "I am convinced, my friends, that water will one day be used as a fuel, that hydrogen and oxygen, its components, will become an inexhaustible source of heat and light, the intensity of which cannot be imagined. Water is the coal of the future."

And how are we doing after about 150 years? For reasons yet to be mentioned, the demand for coal power is currently reaching record levels! In the above book, I present a whole range of new energy technologies, especially those that use water to generate energy, including Schauberger's water home power plant, energy through the power of waves, the Dingel car: water instead of gasoline, Stanley Meyer's water buggy, Genepax & Ricketts: more water cars, LOHC: ingenious hydrogen storage, and many more examples of non-conventional energy use.

Free energy, which we could have had at our disposal more than a hundred years ago thanks to Nikola Tesla, does not suit the multinationals that make horrendous profits from fossil fuels. And so the oil magnates in particular have suppressed free energy projects by compensating their inventors with large sums of money or keeping them from further work with massive threats. When inventors, like Stanley Meyer and many others, do not cooperate, murder is also an option.

What is free energy? The Chinese call it Qi, the Japanese Chi, and the Hindus Prana. The ancient Greeks called it the energy of the vacuum, Reich Orgon, and Nikola Tesla scalar waves. Today we usually call it space or vacuum energy. Viktor Schauberger, one of the most important founders of free energy, wanted to reveal to his fellow men the ancient knowledge of the nature of water in a new way. If we would follow his findings, we would have healthy water and could draw unlimited, clean, and almost free energy from water and air. For this purpose it would be necessary to replace the present death technology of explosion with the biotechnology of implosion; a simple step, in order to solve the largest problems of mankind.

And this is also the reason why everything that would make us independent from the energy industry is suppressed. Free Energy machines were already working about 100 years ago in the Ford T, the first automobile to come off the assembly line. Photos of Magnetos, Nikola Tesla's Free Energy generators, which were installed in the first 40,000 of the successful Ford T model, I have shown in my above-mentioned book. Nikola Tesla's Pierce Arrow is not a legend either! Even if many beneficiaries of the energy economy assign true events from egoistic motives to the area of the conspiracy theory.

How long should real free energy solutions, which could offer energy independence to every individual, be suppressed? How much longer will taxpayers have to give away their hard-earned money for symbolic solutions that do not compete with the status quo, such as wind and solar power? When will the threatening and murdering of the now far more than one hundred ingenious inventors finally stop? In the book mentioned above, you will find some exemplary reports about threatened and murdered inventors by money-corrupted irresponsible people.

Some years ago, when the wellknown space energy expert Prof. Dr. Claus W. Turtur thanked me for my blog report, we had an interesting conversation about the threats. When I told him that I better change the genre in my writing, the dangerously living professor said we could have a chat; with my experiences, you could write an exciting thriller.

Paradigm shift in energy production

Again and again we see, hear or experience effects or consequences which we cannot explain with the established physics. Many of my books are full of such contexts, which I could explain quite simply. The dynamic ether, which also Einstein did not reject, has many names, like dark energy, physical energy, vacuum energy, quintessence, zero-point-energy and so on.

Vortex and spiral structures are the primordial forms occurring at all levels of nature and in laboratories, e. g. the atomic structure, vortex lattice in superconductors, lightning, quasar (star-like radio source), etc. Yet mainstream physics, with its skepticism and blinkered thinking, continues to close its doors to modern physics. Robert B. Laughlin, who received the Nobel Prize in Physics in 1998, says: "You can't study modern physics at any university in the world because everything taught there is one-half disproved and half irrelevant. The relevant physics takes place behind closed doors in the laboratories of armaments and industry. The researchers who work there use laws of nature unknown to (most ed. note) university professors."

In my book "How Water Connects Our Worlds", I reported, among other things, that the Italian Andrea Rossi has succeeded in developing a small reactor that has the potential to heat our buildings in an environmentally friendly and affordable way. Meanwhile, several replications of Andrea Rossi's Ecat have already tested. Prof. Parkhomov published a paper in Russian on another such scale that uses 1.2 grams of hydrogen-saturated nickel powder to produce heat for 225 days. You can keep up with the latest developments regarding LENR energy here: https://coldreaction.net/lenr-die-unendliche-und-saubere-energie-kommtfrueher-als-gedacht.html.

In the article "Physics of Torsion Fields" in raum&zeit No. 219, the graduate engineer Hans Würtz from Bonn, Germany, presents a torsion field motor and thus provides experimental evidence of a previously unknown force, which he identifies as torsion fields. In Russia, the existance of torsion fields is almost part of the established scientific world view. This proven form of radiation can be denied by stubborn individuals at best.

Hans Würtz describes an easy-to-perform experiment that suggests torsion fields. We can replicate his torsion field motor with little effort and check its functionality. It works quite differently from our current combustion and electric motors, namely with torsion fields. The motor de facto needs no energy supply and starts by itself. But it is by no means a perpetual motion machine, because the actual mechanical power, i. e. the energy, comes from the physical vacuum. However, the mechanical output is currently minimal. Torsion fields propagate at least a hundred million times the speed of light. They carry neither mass nor power, but information expressed by the change from left to clockwise rotation and vice versa and by an amplitude ("field strength"). The change takes place without energy but has real effects in the physical vacuum leading to symmetry breaking in it so that we generate real mechanical power and thus energy.

Every object, every element, whether hollow or filled with mass, has its torsion field. There is nothing in nature where torsion fields are not involved. This regularity is valid down to the atomic level. As said before, you can reconstruct the torsion field motor of Hans Würtz based on the drawings in raum&zeit No. 219 with little effort and check its functionality. With the various torsion field motor suggestions, the graduate engineer wants to give the reader an incentive to become active in this field himself. So, all you Gyro Gearheads, get to work! I wish you happy work! https://www.raum-und-zeit.com/r-z-online/artikel-archiv/raum-zeit-heftearchiv/alle-jahrgaenge/2019/ausgabe-219/physik-der-torsionsfelder.html

While the fuel cell principle was discovered as early as 1838 by the German-Swiss chemist and physicist Christian Friedrich Schönbein, its use has been conspicuously limited. Barely 40 years later, when Jules Verne orated that water was the coal of the future, he expressed the hope that sooty steam engines could soon get replaced by the fuel cell. But his predictions would take some 150 years to come true - after all, Europe's northern countries seem to have made the spread of hydrogen electromobility a declared state task. For the German drivers, the dream of mass-produced hydrogen-powered cars does not come true until 2025. Although the Hydrogen 7 or its two predecessors were among the first hydrogen-powered vehicles in the world, built by BMW back in 2000. Mercedes also builds its GLC F-Cell electric SUV with fuel cell and plug-in hybrid technology only for selected customers, such as Deutsche Bahn and the cities of Stuttgart and Hamburg. The Asians will win the race, and the German carmakers will lag far behind. After all, in addition to Honda and Toyota, Hyundai now, also has a genuine hydrogen car in its portfolio. And at 69,000 euros, the Nexo is a fuel cell vehicle that the company offers even more cheaply than its Asian competitors. And unlike the Mercedes model mentioned above, we can buy the Nexo.

My suspicion in the whole matter is that German politics and business are primarily concerned with permanent growth. Just as they now give right of way to battery-powered electric vehicles by hook or crook, so it was with diesel back then. First they let the stupid Michel buy the expensive diesel vehicles and then make him want to buy the next one. When the market saturates with battery-powered e-mobiles, hydrogen cars will go into mass production. And when this market is saturated, the radiation-free and environmentally friendly LOW-NUCLEAR-REACTIONS (LENR) TECHNOLOGY, such as the E-Cat SK, will finally be introduced. And again and again, the Germans will lag behind the Asians in terms of essential components. More on the subject of hydrogen cars and other alternative forms of propulsion can you find, as I said, in my book "How Water Connects Our Worlds".

In the last part of the above mentioned book with the same title, I present new energy technologies and their inventors, especially those who generate energy with water, among others, Schauberger's water home power plant, energy generation through the power of waves, the Dingel car: water instead of gasoline, Stanley Meyer's water buggy, Genepax & Ricketts: more water cars, LOHC: ingenious hydrogen storage and many more examples of non-conventional energy use.

As a physician's assistant in the Odenwald, a certified educator in Frankfurt and a doctor of nutritional sciences in the USA, I always wished to help people become healthy.

In 1997, living again in Germany, I published my study results about Spirulina and the immune system in books from Windpferd Verlag. After some thirty health, lifestyle and water books, I hope my readers can benefit from my research.

Until years ago, I worked with juveniles with behavioral problems in Portugal. After my husband died, I edited books for Jim Humble Publishing for two years. Currently, I daily hike in the mountains, and rescuing free-roaming animals.

Our body and everything around us is vibrating water that responds to voices, moods, and music. The Japanese water researcher Masaru Emoto discovered water molecules changing according to the sounds exposed.

In cooperation with the water artist Ernst Braun, Marianne Meyer found out who realizes water art. She explains her research results comprehensibly, using many partly colored water crystal photos in different tests.

The book leads you on the path into the depths of life and reveals the secret in our genes. By embracing our shadows and realizing how much our trained way of thinking influences us, fear no longer has to impair our mental power in the future. Another content is the principle of shaping our reality by making it clear to ourselves what we want. What we do to make ourselves and others happy is what makes us happy.

The reader also will find disturbing facts about the quality of commercial and tap waters.

Ultimately, the author introduces free energy researchers and their technologies. She also shows what to do, so space energy can soon flow into all households.

ISBN 978-3734736919 104 p. 17x22cm €7,99

We all need Spirulina. Why? Because of infertile soils, we can hardly get energy from our food. The blue-green alga is concentrated solar energy, because it contains all the colors of the spectrum, and hence all the frequencies of light as the warter of Lourdes.

Marianne Erika Meyer introduced "Spirulina, das blaugrüne Wunder" (the blue-green miracle) via her same-named German best-seller and an appearance on Prime TV in German-speaking Europe and Russia.

Evermore folks supplement their diets with beneficial protein food. And dentists use it progressively for discharging amalgam and other toxins.

Stunning studies & reports around the globe prove: With Spirulina, we strengthen our immune system and stand up to pain, depression, diabetes, MS, cataracts, allergies, anemia, arthritis, liver fibrosis, and Parkinson's disease, and even AIDS and cancer.

In the illustrated book with delicious recipes, the Ph.D. nutritionist covered each chapter in note form and highlighted crucial parts.

ISBN 978-3734728525 104 p. 17x22cm €7,99

Marianne E. Meyer

CRANBERRY POWER FRUIT

Handbook to the Methuselah Berry

Sensational Healing Successes and Delicious Recipes for the Healthy Kitchen

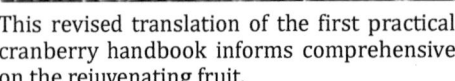

This revised translation of the first practical cranberry handbook informs comprehensive on the rejuvenating fruit.

The expert for natural remedies shows how cranberry is indispensable as natural health care helper. Cranberry prevents the adhesion of bacteria for bladder infections, acute cystitis, and urinary tract infections. It may even represent a promising co-adjuvant for preventing and treating COVID-19. Due to its antithrombotic and anti-inflammatory properties, its resveratrol expects to reduce COVID-19-associated mortality.

Cranberry's best-established medical applications are preventing and treating bacterial infections of the urinary tract, the gastric mucosa and the oral cavity.

This work demonstrates the potential to preventing and curing some 80% of all health problems, including cardiovascular diseases (especially atherosclerosis), rheumatoid arthritis and cancer. We can turn back the clock, reversing premature aging symptoms.

Delicious recipes from Marianne Meyer's health kitchen and trendy cocktails complete the book with the red round power fruit.

ISBN 978-3743181595 104 p. 17x22cm €7,99

In this captivating autobiographical novel, we take part in the author's exciting intercontinental life. It becomes clear that we are all connected and that families have had their value systems for generations.

This code of own rules, idioms and communication styles expresses even when family members live on different continents without knowing each other. The book's first edition was a gift for the author's relative, Doris Day, to show what her grandmother's life might have been like had she not immigrated to the US.

The book also represents a bridge connecting the realm of the living and dead. It shows there is no guilt, chance or luck, only cause and effect, which may be many centuries and incarnations apart. Luck, bad luck and chance are just terms for the law that is not yet recognized. And if you don't learn, you suffer. The only thing that remains is what connects the worlds, the only meaning of life: LOVE.

Reader I. B. G.: "The book clearly conveys lived spirituality and belongs in every household."

At BoD or or other online book stores, you can read part of the book, but for cosmic plus points, it is better to order it from the local bookseller.

ISBN 978-3741282331 184 p. 17x22 cm €8.98